MODERN ECONOMIC ISSUES

OTTO ECKSTEIN, *Harvard University, General Editor*

In this series the great public issues in economics are posed and put in perspective by original commentary and reprints of the most interesting and significant recent statements by experts in economics and government.

ROGER E. BOLTON, the editor of this volume, received his Ph.D. from Harvard University, where he now teaches economics. A student of the problems of regional growth, as well as of the economics of defense and disarmament, Dr. Bolton is the author of the forthcoming *Defense Purchases and Regional Growth.*

DEFENSE AND DISARMAMENT

THE ECONOMICS OF TRANSITION

Edited by Roger E. Bolton

 PRENTICE-HALL, Inc., Englewood Cliffs, N.J.

A SPECTRUM BOOK

To My Wife

To My Wife

CONTENTS

DEFENSE AND DISARMAMENT

The Economics of Transition

INTRODUCTION

DEFENSE SPENDING: BURDEN OR PROP?

Roger E. Bolton

A stranger to our society might be puzzled by our ambivalent attitude toward defense spending. On the one hand, we view defense as a "burden." A significant part of our productive capacity is tied up in this area. It would be much better if we needed less defense and could use our capacity to produce other things instead: automobiles, education, cleaner streets, or more aid to the unfortunate at home or abroad. Defense, however, *is* a necessary burden, and to lighten it we feel we must be economical or efficient in producing it: i.e., use up as few resources as possible.

On the other hand, defense production is viewed as a "prop" for the economy. It furnishes employment for millions of people and is a chief cause of the prosperity of whole industries, regions, and occupations. Without it, would these resources find employment elsewhere? The "burden" notion assumes that they would, but there is also the fear that they would not. What if they were simply to go to waste? Then we would not get the benefits of alternative production after all; worse, there would be the added social evils which accompany unemployment.

Even partial disarmament, then, may appear to be a mixed blessing. If the resources it frees are transferred to other uses, disarmament* will be a great boon, for it will ease Cold War tensions and allow an increase in consumption for all. But if the resources cannot be easily transferred, disarmament will mean distress for those sectors dependent on defense production and—because all parts of the economy are linked together—for others as well.

These fears are not without foundation. One cruel economic reality is that men and capital do not automatically find employ-

---

* The word *disarmament* will be used here to cover any sizable reduction in defense expenditures. The types of problems are the same in any case, although they are naturally more serious the greater the reductions involved.

ment. Resources are employed only when they are in demand, and new demands may not quickly spring up to replace old ones. Deliberate policies are needed to bring about a smooth adjustment to changes in demand. It is imperative, therefore, that the whole society begin to think ahead about disarmament. Thinking ahead does not necessarily mean "planning," with all the bad connotations that word has for many people. (In fact, although the completely laissez-faire economy may adjust to disarmament only slowly and imperfectly, the experiences of some of the planned economies suggest that they would do little better. The reconversion problem may be easiest in a mixed economy, such as that of the United States.) Thinking ahead means delineating the problem in advance, determining the most effective policy "mix," and then setting up machinery for the rapid implementation of that mix when the need arises. It is not wise to wait until the problem arrives, especially since some policy tools are slower in working than the cumulative economic processes which spread and magnify any initial loss in demand.

Another reason for thinking ahead is that such preparation to cope with the problem may actually hasten disarmament. Although the major factor in making negotiated disarmament so difficult to achieve is not economic in nature, it is possible that fear of the adverse economic consequences may contribute to lack of progress. Being prepared for the economic adjustment required may make the world more eager to seek the opportunity to make it. (It is interesting to note the comments of Norman Cousins, in Article 12, along this line.)

It is reassuring to note that such thinking is taking place in the United States today and that the appropriate adjustment responses are being considered. Although disarmament has not been imminent, defense demand seemed to be leveling off, even without a disarmament treaty, until the increase in United States forces in Viet Nam, begun in the summer of 1965. This increase will not and should not eliminate the need for thinking ahead about possible later reductions.

But if the defense budget remains a large burden we must continue to meet defense needs as efficiently as possible. The problem of economizing resources is still vitally important. This is as much an economic problem as disarmament, and it too commands much attention. In fact, a number of innovations in military management, procurement, and budgeting have appeared in recent years. Not all increases in efficiency involve immediate reductions in expenditures. For example, military manpower costs may be raised by increases in pay, which are essential in attracting the competent personnel needed for efficient military management. But many other efficiency measures do involve reductions in expenditures—the closing of bases, the cutting back of certain forces or kinds of equipment, and so on. These selective reductions provide a foretaste of disarmament for sectors that specialize in defense production. They have the salutary effect of hastening studies of the problem and stimulating advance planning. They also have the disturbing effect of spurring use of "politics" in attempts to reverse the reductions. On the other hand, those who protest the reductions do raise the valid point that U.S. Department of Defense activities have repercussions that may negate other federal actions. A base closing, for instance, can cause poverty in an area just as other programs are being introduced to alleviate poverty there. This does not imply efficiency should be compromised; it does mean that efficiency in the defense establishment may not produce cuts in the whole federal budget.

THE GENERAL IMPACT OF DEFENSE ON THE ECONOMY *

Just how great is the impact of the defense effort on the economy as a whole? How much of our total output does it absorb? In short, how big is the "burden"—or the "prop"?

Table 1 gives some pertinent figures for 1955 (the year defense expenditures reached their lowest level in the post-Korean War cutback), 1960 (the year marking a temporary halt in the renewed buildup after 1955), and 1963 (the most recent year for which comparable data are available). The table reveals that national defense expenditures have been a significant fraction of our gross national product (GNP), the total output of the economy, and an even larger share of total federal expenditures.

* The data on GNP and its components used in this book are from the U.S. Department of Commerce series as published before the official August 1965 revisions. These revisions, however, had relatively little effect on the magnitudes discussed in the book.

Table 1

National Defense Expenditures: 1955, 1960, 1963
(in billions of dollars)

Year	1955	1960	1963
GNP	397.5	502.6	583.9
Total federal expenditures*	68.9	93.1	115.2
National defense expenditures			
Military services and foreign			
military assistance	37.5	43.7	51.0
Atomic energy development	1.7	2.7	3.0
Miscellaneous**	.8	.1	.2
Total	40.0	46.5	54.2
National defense as a percentage of GNP	10.1	9.3	9.3

* National Income Accounts Basis. See *The Budget of the United States Government, 1966* (Washington, D.C.: USGPO, 1965), Special Analysis A, p. 356, for definition and coverage.

** Chiefly stockpiling and the financing of defense production facilities. The 1955 figure also includes nonmilitary expenditures for space exploration.

Source: U.S. Department of Commerce, *Survey of Current Business* (Washington, D.C.: USGPO, July 1964), pp. 20-21, and *U.S. Income and Output* (Washington, D.C.: USGPO, 1958), p. 175.

Defense expenditures, however, have recently been growing more slowly than GNP. After 1962, defense spending leveled off and then began to decline slightly, while GNP continued to grow rapidly. The Viet Nam build-up will reverse the decline, at least temporarily, but the rise in the percentage of GNP may be very slight.

The leveling off of the rise in expenditures reflects the completion of a new military buildup initiated by the Kennedy Administration. The slight easing of international tensions also contributed to this leveling off. A trend toward higher military pay and pensions is offset by a very determined cost-cutting campaign in the Department of Defense. Secretary of Defense Robert McNamara set a goal of $4 billion in annual savings by fiscal year 1967,[1] a goal to be achieved without reducing the amount of defense protection.

But forecasting defense expenditures for more than a few years ahead is very hazardous indeed. Anticipated declines may turn out to be temporary, like those of 1955 and 1960. International developments and advances in military technology cannot be predicted. In 1964 Roswell G. Gilpatric, former Deputy Secretary of Defense, noted that the possibility of a true understanding between the United States and the Soviet Union might lower the level of defense needs about 25 per cent below that of fiscal year 1964.[2] This statement attracted much attention and made many people aware, for the first time, of the considerable chances for future reductions in defense expenditures. The 25 per cent figure, in fact, has been quoted frequently without mention of the many *if*'s in the original statement.

Table 2 presents those defense expenditures which involve pur-

Table 2

National Defense Purchase-Type Expenditures: 1955, 1960, 1963
(in billions of dollars)

Year	1955	1960	1963
GNP	397.5	502.6	583.9
Federal purchases of goods and services	45.3	53.1	64.7
Federal purchases for military services and foreign military assistance			
Military wages and salaries	9.8	9.9	10.9
Civilian wages and salaries	4.8	5.7	6.5
Construction	1.3	1.4	1.6
Military equipment	13.3	14.7	17.6
Other goods and services	7.5	11.0	13.0
Total	36.7	42.7	49.5
Atomic energy development	1.6	2.3	2.3
Miscellaneous*	.8	.1	.2
Total	39.1	45.2	52.1

* See Footnote ** in Table 1.
Source: U.S. Department of Commerce, *Survey of Current Business* (Washington, D.C.: USGPO, July 1964), p. 22, and *U.S. Income and Output* (Washington, D.C.: USGPO, 1958), p. 178.

chases of goods and services, excluding such costs as outright grants and pensions. Because defense expenditures, unlike other federal expenditures, are almost wholly composed of such purchases, the totals in Table 2 are close to those given in Table 1. Corresponding detail for 1964 is not yet available, but total defense purchases declined by nearly one billion dollars from 1963.

Almost one third of all defense costs are composed of wages and salaries (including subsistence and other allowances to military personnel). The numbers of people involved indicate the size of the military establishment, as shown in Table 3.

Table 3

Defense Establishment Employees: 1955, 1960, 1963

Year	Active-Duty Military Personnel	Civilian Employees	Total
1955	2,935,100	1,180,100	4,115,200
1960	2,476,400	1,047,000	3,523,400
1963	2,699,700	1,058,000	3,757,700

Source: U.S. Civil Service Commission, *Monthly Report on Federal Employment* (Washington, D.C.: USGPO), various issues, and U.S. Bureau of the Census, *Statistical Abstract of the United States* (Washington, D.C.: USGPO, 1964). Military personnel as of June 30th of each year; civilian employees as of December 31st. Civilian employees include those in the Department of Defense, the Selective Service System, the Atomic Energy Commission, and the Office of Emergency Planning.

Some readers may be surprised at the large number of civilian employees in defense agencies. They constitute about 40 per cent of all federal employees. In 1963 about 10 per cent of these civilian workers were employed abroad; only about 80,000 worked in the Washington, D.C., metropolitan area. Civilians work in every imaginable capacity, from janitors and unskilled clerical workers to scientists, engineers, and executives—even funeral directors. Nearly 100,000 work in the naval shipyards, and many more are employed in other industrial facilities, such as arsenals, printing plants, and maintenance depots.

The U.S. Bureau of Labor Statistics estimated that in 1963 there were just under 3 million employees in defense production in private industry. Table 4 shows the distribution according to industry.

If the 3 million are added to the military and civilian personnel in the defense establishment itself, the total for 1963 is about 6.7 million. This was about 9 per cent of all the employment in the

Table 4

Percentage Distribution of Defense Employees in Private Industry

Aircraft and parts	20
Ship- and boat-building	3
Other transportation equipment	5
Electrical equipment and supplies	18
Ordnance and accessories (including missile work)	9
Other	45
Total	100

Source: Joseph F. Fulton, "Employment Impact of Changing Defense Programs," *Monthly Labor Review* (May 1964), 508.

economy (or nearly the same proportion of the labor force as defense expenditures were of GNP).

THE GENERAL PROBLEM OF DISARMAMENT

The unmistakable impression is that defense production looms large in the national economy, be it burden or prop. If defense production could be reduced, the freed resources would permit a significant increase in the production of consumer goods or capital goods. The exact proportions that would be used for present versus future consumption, and for private versus public consumption, are important issues. But there could be a large increase all around. The opportunities now forgone in favor of arms production constitute the cost or burden which must be shouldered today.

But the opportunities depend on the economic potential actually being exploited in civilian production. This requires, almost surely, positive government action to encourage and permit new private demands and/or to supply demand directly by government purchases. Both recent practice and the Full Employment Act of 1946, which commits the government to maintain general economic stability, suggest that appropriate policies would, in fact, be implemented: tax cuts, increased nondefense expenditures, easier money policies, and so forth. These could provide enough demand *in the aggregate* to offset the decline in defense demand.

An aggregate offset, however, is not sufficient to insure a smooth conversion in case of disarmament. Trouble can arise if the product composition of the new demand is much different from that of the defense demand, and if the resources are not easily convertible from one kind of production to the other. If the newly freed resources available are appropriate only for producing X—a certain kind of weapon—then stimulating the demand for Y—some consumer good—will not solve the problem. Not only will the men, machines, and knowledge formerly producing X now go unemployed, but the demand for Y may exceed production capacity. Such excess demand will dissipate itself more in increased prices than in increased production. The result will be the worst possible combination: unemployment along with inflation. The avoidance of this situation may be called the "structural" problem of disarmament, as contrasted to the aggregate offset problem.

The policy implications of these dangers will be discussed later. For the present, however, an analysis of the product mix of defense spending may provide a perspective on the importance of the structural problem. What goods do the military services buy? Would these goods find civilian markets after disarmament? If not, are they produced by firms which can easily convert to the production of civilian goods? Which resources—capital, labor, know-how —would face the greatest problems?

THE SPECIALIZATION OF DEFENSE RESOURCES

Everyone knows that some of the resources currently employed in defense production are so specialized they largely depend on defense production for current employment (the whole aircraft-missiles industrial complex, for example). The concentration of these resources in particular geographical regions intensifies the problem, because mobility is harder over long distances than from industry to industry over a short distance. We may distinguish two kinds of specialization. One is *industrial specialization*, which refers to firms, industries, and occupations specialized in defense. The other is *regional specialization*, which refers to the direct or indirect dependence of many firms in a region, regardless of their products, on military demand. Mobility and reconversion are the most difficult when both types of specialization are present.

Industrial and regional specialization are significant enough to suggest sizable structural problems during and after disarmament. But not all firms and employees involved in military production will have an appreciable adjustment problem, if there is a generally full-employment economy. They are versatile, or else their products would be very much in demand for civilian markets as well. A comment by then Deputy Secretary of Defense Gilpatric in 1963 is enlightening:

A basic fact about the structure of the defense budget and the kind of economic impacts that flow from it is that the greater part of the defense budget is spent for products and services which differ either not at all or not fundamentally from the products used in the civilian economy or for products and services which, although clearly for "military" end use, employ technologies and skills which have ready applications in nondefense markets.

Specifically, about $30 billion, out of a roughly $50 billion defense budget, goes for things not markedly—or often not at all—different from ordinary nondefense markets. . . . Only about $20 billion goes for uniquely military hard goods. Even in this category a large share—perhaps half or more—goes for products whose manufacturers could, provided the economy was firm, readily convert to civilian markets, as was so successfully done following World War II and the Korean War. I refer here not only to producers of items with commercial counterparts, such as trucks and transport planes, but even to producers of many components of missile, nuclear, and other weapons systems. A reasonable estimate might be $10 billion as the "hard-core" military sector of the economy which would be hard to change over to civilian uses, as against $40 billion which is either civilian in nature to begin with or reasonably convertible to nondefense uses.[3]

Whether or not this is too optimistic an appraisal depends partly on what we demand in the way of speed and smoothness of transition after reductions in defense spending. The quicker the adjustment we demand, the greater is the problem posed by the specialization of defense resources. Policy standards will reflect acceptable combinations of price rises and unemployment. For example, the policy may be to try to keep the unemployment rate below 4.5 per cent, not allowing it to rise above that level for more than a few months at a time. Or, the maximum acceptable rate of price increase arising from sectoral shifts in demand may be set at 2 per cent for one year. These hypothetical targets are suggested only to illustrate the dimensions involved; different standards will require different policies.

Let us consider various categories of defense expenditures and the related questions of convertibility and specialization. Initially, we shall confine ourselves to industrial conversion, leaving the regional adjustment problems until later.

Military Personnel

Military personnel refers to the enlisted men and officers who will return to the civilian labor force. What kinds of labor resources do they represent?

A modern military force requires specialists, trained for sophisticated occupations. To a striking degree, the Armed Forces rely on

Table 5

Percentage Distribution, by Educational Level, of Armed Forces Personnel and of Employed Male Civilians: 1960*

Years of Schooling Completed	Ages 18-24		Ages 25-34	
	Armed Forces	Civilians	Armed Forces	Civilians
Elementary school:				
Less than eight years	1.4	8.5	3.4	11.0
Eight years	3.9	7.5	7.0	9.6
High school:				
One to three years	26.2	26.1	22.3	21.5
Four years	51.8	38.4	43.3	30.6
College:				
One to three years	10.7	14.9	11.5	11.9
Four years or more	6.0	4.6	12.5	15.4
Total	100.0	100.0	100.0	100.0

* Armed Forces personnel based in the United States.
Source: 1960 Census of Population, *Educational Attainment*, p. 54; presented in U.S. Senate Committee on Labor and Public Welfare, *Convertibility of Space and Defense Resources to Civilian Needs* (Washington, D.C.: USGPO, 1964), p. 632.

military specialists. Increasingly complicated weapons require spe-cial skills to operate and maintain as well as to manufacture. So trends in military occupations partly parallel those in civilian fields. Although this specialization may create structural problems, the potential job-seekers will at least have had education and training in some area of modern technology. It is sometimes thought that many men are in the Armed Forces only because they could not find a job elsewhere. If this is true, it is because of generally high unemployment, not because they lack fitness for civilian jobs. It usually turns out that the "unemployables" are also unsuited for military service—they are the rejectees who have become the objects of so much concern. They will continue to be special prob-lems, disarmament or no.

Census statistics on the education of Armed Forces personnel in 1960 are shown in Table 5. In terms of high school completion, for example, Armed Forces personnel are significantly ahead of em-ployed male civilians; in terms of higher education, they are not far behind.

Table 6 illustrates occupation trends, revealing the startling fact that, in the Armed Forces, electronics specialists now outnumber infantrymen.

Table 6

*Trends in Occupations of Enlisted Personnel**

	Percentage of Total		
Occupational Group	End of World War II	Korean War	Fiscal Year 1963
Electronics	6.0	10.0	14.4
Crafts and services	26.7	22.7	19.1
Clerical	15.3	20.8	19.8
Other technicians and mechanics	28.4	29.1	32.5
Ground combat	23.6	17.4	14.2
Total	100.0	100.0	100.0

* Excludes recruits, trainees, seamen, and other positions without specific occupational designation.

Source: U.S. Senate Committee on Labor and Public Welfare, *Convertibility of Space and Defense Resources to Civilian Needs* (Washington, D.C.: USGPO, 1964), p. 629.

Norman Paul, Assistant Secretary of Defense for Manpower, points out that released military personnel may adjust more easily to defense reductions than certain civilian groups:

First, military personnel must, because of the very nature of the military mission, be capable of fulfilling a variety of duties at all times. . . . They must, moreover, be capable of performing these duties under many types of adverse conditions only rarely found in civilian pursuits. As a result, individuals with certain physical or mental limitations, who can readily perform some specialized or routine duties in civilian life, may not be capable of being used in military service. . . . Secondly, unlike the civilian labor force, the peacetime military job structure makes little or no provision for the unskilled worker as such. The types of duties performed by the laborer or unskilled service worker are normally performed by personnel in their first years of service, including recent recruits and trainees. These men are, at the same time, serving an apprenticeship or acquiring on-the-job training in a particular military occupation. There is no room in our peacetime force structure for the untrained filler or the career private.[4]

The relative youth of enlisted personnel should also help to make them adaptable. Older officers may be less adaptable, but many of them would be retained as cadres even if the Armed Forces were to be drastically reduced.

Civilian Employees of the Armed Forces

The occupations represented here are of tremendous variety. Although it is hard to generalize, most civilian employees of the defense establishment—except those who are overly concentrated in specific geographical areas—would probably find adjustment relatively easy. In many cases, their present occupations are similar to those in the civilian sector or in other parts of government. If these sectors expand, transfers will be relatively easy in large and diversified cities. There are exceptions, however: some government employees work at very specialized trades in industrial-type establishments; others lack adaptability because of age. Recently formulated plans to close some naval shipyards have brought the problems faced by their workers to national attention.

The general conclusions just drawn are supported by the data in

Table 7

*Distribution of Total White-Collar and Blue-Collar Employees
by Occupation: 1960**

Occupation Group	Percentage of Total Employees
White-collar	50.8
General administrative, clerical, and office services	18.2
Supply	6.4
Engineering	6.3
Accounting and budget	4.5
Business-type management and procurement administration	2.5
Mathematics, statistics, and sciences	2.1
Personnel	1.8
Education	1.4
Medical and health	.9
Transportation	.8
Other	6.0
Blue-collar	49.2
Industrial equipment operation and maintenance	9.6
Metal- and machine-shop work	7.6
Electrical, electronics, and instrumental operation and maintenance	6.2
Warehousing, packing, and processing	6.0
Woodworking, pipefitting, painting, and construction	5.6
Aircraft repair	3.4
Manual labor	3.2
Marine operations	2.2
Services	2.0
Other	3.4
Total	100.0

* As of October 31, 1960. Data cover a total of 958,697 employees. Items have been rounded.
Source: U.S. Civil Service Commission, *Occupations of Federal White-Collar Workers, As of October 31, 1960,* and *Occupations of Federal Blue-Collar Workers, As of October 31, 1960* (Washington, D.C.: USGPO, 1963).

Table 7, which gives a breakdown of blue-collar and white-collar employees of the Armed Forces in 1960. It covers about 960,000 employees, or 90 per cent of all civilian workers in defense-related agencies in 1960, and was prepared from more detailed reports.

Procurement

The third and largest category of purchases is procurement. This includes payments to private firms for military equipment, supplies, and services, construction, and research and development. The kinds of things bought are revealed in Table 8, which shows a

Table 8

Military Prime Contract Awards, by Program: 1964*

Program	Value (in millions of dollars)	Percentage of Total to Business Firms for Work in the U. S.
Intragovernmental	562	
Work outside U.S.	1,326	
Educational and nonprofit Institutions	688	
Business firms for work in the U.S.	26,221	100.0
Major hard goods		
Aircraft	6,067	23.1
Missile systems	5,579	21.3
Ships	1,485	5.7
Tank-automotive	745	2.9
Weapons	211	.8
Ammunition	661	2.5
Electronics and communications equipment	2,918	11.1
Services	1,800	6.9
All other		
Subsistence	579	2.2
Textiles, clothing, and equipage	262	1.0
Fuels and lubricants	788	3.0
Miscellaneous hard goods	1,054	4.0
Construction	1,360	5.2
All awards of less than $10,000	2,710	10.3
Total	28,796	

* Items have been rounded.
Source: U.S. Department of Defense, *Military Prime Contract Awards and Subcontract Payments or Commitments, July-September 1964* (Washington, D.C.: Office of the Secretary of Defense, 1964).

classification of defense contracts in fiscal year 1964 by "procurement program." These data include procurement by Department of Defense research and industrial installations, but not by the Atomic Energy Commission or the National Aeronautics and Space Administration.

The importance of aircraft, missiles, and electronics systems is obvious. There is little chance that civilian demand alone would support the present volume of producton in these areas, even with generous allowances for the expansion of civilian space exploration, commercial air travel, rocket mail delivery, and the like. Certainly many specialized electronics components now produced for the military would have no market after disarmament. Difficulty is also certain for ship-building, weapons, and ammunition firms, because their products are very much less in demand for civilian use. The producers of tank-automotive equipment would perhaps be in less difficult straits, because their skills and capacity are to some extent transferrable to civilian automobile and truck production.

The other items in the table are generally similar to products turned out for consumer and private investment demand and should easily find civilian markets. Many of them require no special fabrication or specifications. But again there is the regional problem: suppliers may find adjustment difficult because they are located in regions where defense installations or contractors are the major buyers in the market.

Given the composition of the military budget, it is not surprising that certain industries are heavily dependent on military orders. The U.S. Bureau of Labor Statistics estimated that 95 per cent of the employees in the ordnance industry (including guided missiles) and about 90 per cent of those in the aircraft industry were engaged in defense production in 1963. Fifty per cent or more of the employees in the communications equipment, electronic components, and ship-building industries were so engaged. About 80 per cent of the employees in these five industries combined were estimated to be engaged in defense production.[5]

Nor is it surprising to find individual firms dependent on defense orders for most of their business. These firms are discussed by Murray Weidenbaum (Article 5). This dependence is a prime cause of regional specialization because some areas are dominated by a few large firms.

Research and development are also important in defense procurement. Of the total value of prime contracts granted in fiscal year 1964, 20.3 per cent were for research and development (90 per cent of all contracts with educational and nonprofit institutions were for such work). The term *research and development* here includes much of weapons testing and some actual fabrication of advanced weapons not yet perfected. The importance of research and development illustrates the very advanced nature of much defense work. Not only do some firms specialize in unique weapons, but some specialize in weapons not yet in existence. This remoteness from any immediate civilian applications is another problem defense resources would have in converting to nondefense markets.

Of the large defense industries, electronics would seem to have the best chance of maintaining present levels of activity after disarmament. Certain kinds of electronic equipment usable only by the military—e.g., fire-control mechanisms for weapons—would, of course, find no market. But a firm's general competence may be applied to newer products, such as automated control systems in industry or transportation, medical instruments, space exploration, and the like.

The aircraft and missile firms, and their specialized suppliers, will perhaps face the major problems raised by industrial specialization. The Weidenbaum paper and the Lockheed Aircraft Corporation's statement (Article 6) analyze the possibilities of this sector. Their general conclusion is that transfer to civilian production will be difficult, unless there is extensive government assistance. The firms are inexperienced in diversification, concentrate on skills valued by the military but too costly for most civilian applications, and lack extensive competitive marketing experience. There are, however, new products that such firms—given time and federal support—would have a good chance of developing successfully. Many of these are very advanced and costly systems that would be even marginally profitable only if partly financed by the government.

Even if companies could not make a smooth transition, individual employees might—if there were no regional concentration of the aircraft-missiles-electronics complex. Employees of specialized firms in Chicago, for example, will presumably have an easier time finding new jobs than those in Los Angeles or Seattle or Denver. In broadly diversified areas like Chicago, there are other firms to go to; this would be less true in heavily defense-oriented areas like southern California, Seattle, or Denver.

Here is, once again, the regional problem. Regional specialization, in making transfer of individual workers difficult, puts an even greater burden on adjustment by firms. Although difficult, this kind of adjustment may be easier than the interregional movement of individuals. If firms find new demand, regardless of how far away it originates, their adjustment will be eased. Physical distance is a smaller problem for such firms, particularly because they have experience in turning out products of high value, per unit of weight, for which transportation costs are relatively unimportant.

THE REGIONAL IMPACT OF DEFENSE

The regional distribution of defense purchases can only be estimated, but it is certainly uneven. The national average of nearly 10 per cent is misleading in this respect, for some large areas depend on defense activity for a third or more of their employment while others are scarcely affected.

The exact distribution is difficult to determine mainly because of lack of data on the procurement aspect of purchases. The company that assembles the final product does not produce all the value. In fact, the average value produced in the contractor's own plant seems to be about 50 per cent of the total value. The other half represents goods and services produced by other firms and then purchased by the prime contractor. There are data on the distribution of prime contracts by state, but the subcontractors and suppliers may be located in many other states. Their distribution by region has to be estimated in some way. We shall discuss some of these estimates, but for the present even the distribution of prime contracts is instructive. Although it may furnish a misleading picture of the distribution of defense production, it does show the regional pattern of final assembly. This is important because the firms involved in final assembly may be more specialized and thus find adjustment to shifts in demand more difficult. Parts and materials suppliers, on the other hand, may be more versatile, their products being more like the components in products needed to satisfy civilian demand. An electronics tube has a number of uses; a complete Polaris submarine has but one.

Figures on the regional distribution of prime contracts show two important things: it differs from that of population or of economic activity in general; and it has experienced a profound shift since the Korean War—a shift largely resulting from changes in the nature of military weapons. Table 9 shows the data on prime contracts for the Korean War period and for fiscal year 1964. Anyone familiar with the general regional pattern of employment will see the first of the above points; the second is very obvious.

The changes in various states' shares of contract value were also extremely large. Big increases came especially for California, but also for Missouri, Texas, Florida, Virginia, Georgia, Colorado, Arizona, and Utah. Large declines were suffered by Michigan, Indiana, Illinois, Ohio, Wisconsin, Kansas, and New York. Some of these changes came soon after the Korean War; others occurred somewhat later.

Table 9

Distribution of Prime Contract Value among Regions:
Korean War Period and Fiscal Year 1964

	Percentage of Total U.S. Contract Value	
Region	Fiscal Years 1951-53	Fiscal Year 1964
New England	8.1	9.5
Middle Atlantic	25.1	17.6
East North Central	27.4	11.3
West North Central	6.8	9.0
South Atlantic	7.6	13.1
East South Central	1.7	2.4
West South Central	4.7	6.6
Mountain	.7	4.3
Pacific	17.9	26.2
Total	100.0	100.0

Source: U.S. Department of Defense, *The Changing Patterns of Defense Procurement* (Washington, D.C.: Office of the Secretary of Defense, 1962), and *Prime Contract Awards by State, Fiscal Year 1964* (Washington, D.C.: Office of the Secretary of Defense, 1964).

Table 8 gave a breakdown of contracts by kind of item for fiscal year 1964. In a different way, Table 10 compares the composition

Table 10

Composition of Military Hard-Goods Purchases:
Korean War Period and Fiscal Year 1964

	Percentage of U.S. Total*	
Type	*Fiscal Years 1951-53*	*Fiscal Year 1964*
Aircraft	31.5	32.4
Missiles	.5	29.8
Ships	6.8	7.9
Electronics	11.2	15.6
Tank—Automotive, Weapons, Ammunition, Production Equipment, and Miscellaneous	50.0	14.3
Total	100.0	100.0

* Total deliveries of hard goods during the 1951-53 period, and the value of prime contracts let to business firms for hard goods during fiscal year 1964. Hard goods include all items except services, subsistence, clothing, fuels, and construction.

Source: U.S. Department of Defense, *The Changing Patterns of Defense Procurement* (Washington, D.C.: Office of the Secretary of Defense, 1962), and *Military Prime Contract Awards and Subcontract Payments or Commitments, June-September 1964* (Washington, D.C.: Office of the Secretary of Defense, 1964).

of military contracts in fiscal year 1964 with that of the Korean War period. It shows a shift away from products in which the Midwest and the East had largest capacity—vehicles, weapons, and equipment items—toward newer and more complex items, such as missiles and electronics. For various reasons, other parts of the country proved more suitable for this kind of production. The center of the aircraft industry has long been California, and that industry took the lead in developing the new weapons. The emphasis on air and missile warfare also made the South and West desirable for their favorable locations, climates, and open spaces. Some areas had taken part in early research and development efforts which led to later production orders. The Midwest has had a far smaller share of this research and development than might be expected, in view of its university resources.[6] Also, the older industries of the Midwest felt little pressure to keep up with new military developments after the Korean War, because they had prospects of ample markets for their traditional consumer and capital goods. For the aircraft firms, however, it was vital to develop the kinds of products military buyers wanted.

The distribution of military and civilian payrolls also shifted in the decade after the Korean War. This was less pronounced than the shift in the distribution of procurement, nor were the two patterns parallel. But the Middle Atlantic and Midwest regions suffered a loss in payrolls, too, especially in civilian payrolls—a loss that reflected declines in employment in such industrial-type installations as shipyards and arsenals.

Elsewhere, I have estimated the regional distribution of total defense production and used the estimates to draw conclusions regarding the dependence of various regions on defense income and its impact on regional growth.[7] For procurement estimates, this required adjustment of prime contract values to allow for assumed patterns of subcontracting across state lines (the word *subcontracting* here covers all purchases by prime contractors from suppliers). These procurement estimates were then added to figures on military and civilian payrolls to calculate total defense production.

The estimates are available for 1962 and earlier years. They show significantly higher shares (compared to procurement contract shares alone) for the East North Central region and lower ones for the Pacific Coast states. This reflects the fact that much of an item completed in defense-oriented regions is really produced in other areas and shipped as parts and materials to the final assembly areas. These production estimates, however, confirm the great shifts in regional distribution after the Korean War.

To assess the dependence of a region on defense demand, one might express defense income as a percentage of total income—specifically personal income, that being the only comprehensive income measure available for regions. This method, however, ignores the "multiplier" effects of defense income. The multiplier concept focuses on a division of activity in a region into two parts: exogenous, or "outside" income, and total income. Outside income results from demand for the region's products from other regions or payments to it by other regions; exports to other regions, income from property owned outside the region by its residents, and certain transfer payments are the chief sources of this inflow. Defense income is an obvious part. Local income, on the other hand, comes from production of goods and services for local use. As used in the study referred to, the multiplier approach assumes that local production is passive and increases only if exogenous income does. This response brings a multiple effect of changes in defense or any other exogenous income; when a defense plant worker is newly hired, he respends some of his wages on local products and thus indirectly supports new local employment and income. Conversely, if defense demand falls off, the effects—unless offset by some new exogenous demand—are not only lost employment in defense plants, but also losses in local production and income. Therefore, the dependence of a region on defense income is underestimated if it is measured by the ratio to personal income of defense income alone.

The study referred to attempted to take into account these multiplier effects, both for the estimates of defense dependence and for the contribution of defense to growth. Columns 1 and 2 of Table 11 present the dependence estimates for 1962 and the contribution to growth estimates for the 1952-62 period, respectively. Negative numbers for the Column 2 indicate that defense income declined —absolutely, not just relatively—during the period, and thus had a depressing influence which had to be overcome for any growth at all to take place.

The table shows the diverse impact of defense demand. The Middle Atlantic and East North Central regions suffered depressing effects on growth. Having already lost much defense-related activity, however, these areas were correspondingly less dependent on it by 1962. The Mountain and Pacific regions, on the other hand, were more dependent in 1962, after a growth in defense activity which contributed a good deal to growth in general. Some regions were rather dependent both in 1952 and 1962; the intervening period saw changes in the kinds of defense production, but less rapid growth in its total than in the Mountain and Pacific regions.

Table 11 shows a general, but far from perfect, correlation between the impact of defense and the rate of growth actually

Table 11

The Importance of Defense Demand in Various Regions

Region	Contribution of Defense Income		Growth Rates, 1952-62, (percentage per year)	
	To Current Personal Income, 1962 (Percentage of Income)	*To Growth in Personal Income, 1952-62 (Percentage of Growth)*	*Total Personal Income*	*Per Capita Personal Income*
	(1)	*(2)*	*(3)*	*(4)*
New England	22	13	4.8	3.4
Middle Atlantic	16	-3	4.6	3.3
East North Central	12	-21	4.3	2.6
West North Central	13	8	4.5	3.5
South Atlantic	23	13	5.7	3.6
East South Central	16	9	4.7	4.0
West South Central	19	11	4.7	3.1
Mountain	23	27	6.3	2.7
Pacific	34	21	6.4	3.1

Source: Roger E. Bolton, *Defense Purchases and Regional Growth* (Washington, D.C.: The Brookings Institution, forthcoming).

achieved in personal income (compare Columns 2 and 3). Regions which benefitted greatly from defense seemed to grow more rapidly in total income than other regions. This suggests at least some tendency for defense to be a net stimulus, not merely replacing some other activity. However, there is much uncertainty about this. Some areas undoubtedly would have grown rapidly even without defense demand, by basing growth on some other exogenous demand. And it should be noted that all regions managed to grow, although the region with the largest defense losses (East North Central) grew most slowly over the 1952-62 period.

There is, however, almost no relationship between defense impact and growth in per capita income. This is shown by Columns 2 and 4 of Table 11. Regions most stimulated by defense had much lower per capita growth rates than some other regions. It appears that defense demand stimulated growth in total activity in certain regions, including some which had previously been sparsely settled, but that it induced large population increases as well. However, it is again suggestive that the East North Central region had a low rate of growth in per capita income as well.

The experience of the various states within a region is, of course, not uniform. The dependence of certain states on defense is much greater than the regional figures indicate. In 1962, for example, the estimated figures were 25 per cent or more for Maryland, Virginia, Colorado, Utah, Washington, California, Alaska, and Hawaii.[8] Many other states had figures well over 15 per cent. For some metropolitan areas the relative dependence is even higher. The paper by Charles Tiebout (Article 7) gives 1960 estimates for such dependence on defense and space expenditures combined for three cities: Los Angeles-Long Beach, 44 per cent; San Francisco-Oakland, 16 per cent; Seattle, 42 per cent. Other metropolitan areas which have more than average dependence on defense are Denver, St. Louis, Long Island, and Washington, D.C., although in the last case the city proper seems less dependent than adjacent areas in Maryland and Virginia. Until a few years ago, Wichita would have had to be included, but more recently defense production has declined substantially there. (It is important to note that the city has weathered this loss fairly well and is not in a depressed condition.[9]) Neither is the problem limited to large metropolitan areas. Quite a few smaller cities are heavily dependent on defense installations, such as bases and arsenals.

The varying impact of defense on various geographical areas suggests that large reductions in defense expenditures could cause significant problems of structural adjustment. Especially at the city level, there is significant regional specialization, making adjustment difficult without some very specific alternative demands which offset, naturally or through government policies, a loss in defense demand.

Some areas dependent on defense, like some firms and industries, have a limited comparative advantage in the goods and services which would be in growing demand after disarmament. Some areas have achieved their present level of economic development only because of their defense history. In some cases they were literally created out of nothing, because the sites had some special suitability for defense installations or plants. At any rate, they are now large and prosperous communities. And, as Tiebout points out in his essay, the defense support for them has been long-term in nature. There are long-term investment commitments in housing and in commercial and public facilities. These are not temporary concentrations, so the situation of these areas is much different and more difficult than it was in many defense-dependent areas just after World War II. This makes personal losses potentially much greater and reduces mobility which might otherwise hasten the required transition. In another sense, however, the capital formation of the past does make it easier to attract new industries. Not all the community's resources are overspecialized—its schools, streets, and residences can be as useful in supporting one kind of industry as another. The area will thus have an easier time attracting nondefense industry than if it had not been developed at all.

But problems will remain. Some capital and labor will be overspecialized, and the attraction of other industries to certain areas will be difficult because of their limited natural advantages in raw materials, transportation, and accessibility to markets.

Although it will be hard enough for specialized regions to maintain former levels of employment in case of disarmament, it will be even harder for them to achieve past rates of *growth*. If the post-Korean War changes have altered the growth experience of various areas, disarmament could alter it further. And the areas benefitting earlier may now be the ones adversely affected. It may be desirable for government to give special support, perhaps through tax relief or subsidies, to areas most affected, if temporarily necessary to prevent complete waste of resources and to alleviate personal hardship. It would not be desirable, however, for government to provide the artificial demands necessary to maintain rapid growth. Even the steps to maintain former levels of income are proper only if they are of a temporary nature; the government, in fact, may be employing other policies to induce movement of resources out of the affected areas and thus causing long-term declines in these areas.

Defense and Research and Development[10]

The defense effort is the largest single reason for the very large amount invested in research and development each year. National Science Foundation data for 1961-62 show that about $15 billion was being spent each year for the nation as a whole, and that the federal government provided approximately two thirds of these funds. In turn, about two thirds of the federal contribution came in the form of defense contracts, with an additional amount coming from the Atomic Energy Commission. In more recent years, however, support by the National Aeronautics and Space Administration has been growing faster.

The possibility of disarmament raises the question: can the research and development resources be converted to civilian uses and, if so, can this be done without a great increase in government-financed civilian research programs? Such increases, of course, may be desired anyway. An expansion of public education may also be thought desirable, and that could absorb many scientists, as teachers, released from defense production.

It seems probable that civilian-oriented research and development would increase considerably with disarmament, whether privately or publicly financed. The higher priorities of defense research have probably slowed the growth of nondefense work. Although military research and development has had some "fallout" effects in terms of new civilian products, such as the commercial jet airliner, the largest part of such efforts is directed to specifically military items. A reduction in defense needs would therefore allow more research to be directed to civilian purposes, either by freeing government funds for direct sponsorship or by removing forces bidding up the costs of research personnel beyond the competitive range of educational institutions and nondefense industries.

Richard Nelson (Article 8) examines in more detail the impact of defense, and the possible impact of disarmament, on research and development.

Experience with Previous Reductions in Defense Expenditures[11]

In recent years there have been three instances of reductions in defense demand with major impact on the economy. We shall summarize these experiences briefly, drawing conclusions on the possible impact of future reductions and the appropriate policies to deal with them. Each of the previous cases was unique, however, as would be a future one, so only broad implications can be drawn.

The three cases, in order of occurrence as well as of magnitude, are: the extensive disarmament after World War II; the large cutback after the Korean War; and the temporary decline in defense orders in 1957.

It should be noted that changes in defense *expenditures* do not adequately represent the timing or extent of the impact of changes in defense demand. Monetary payments for defense goods are often not made until after much of the actual employment involved has already taken place. In times of rising demand as well as in times of falling demand, the movement of purchases lags behind that of defense-related employment. One needs to look at another indicator: defense orders, or contracts. Orders, too, may be a deficient indicator in themselves, because they usually precede the real impact. But declining orders are important signals to firms, which may begin to make their responses—reducing inventories and employment—even while purchases (or payments) for items still being completed and delivered remain stable.[12] Analysis of the impact of defense demand must sometimes use data on both defense orders and defense purchases.

The Post-World War II Decline

The great reductions after World War II had only a brief deleterious impact on the economy as a whole. The cutback was rapid as well as great, and in both dimensions was far more severe than a future reduction would be. Yet the economy weathered it with flying colors. Nevertheless, the transition did have an unsatisfactory element which should be avoided in the future. Also, the disarmament took place in circumstances overwhelmingly favorable to an easy transition, far more favorable than they would be for a reduction in the near future.

Defense purchases declined from $75.9 billion in 1945 to $18.8 billion in 1946 and then to $11.4 billion in 1947, before beginning a slight rise which continued until just before the Korean hostilities. The Armed Forces numbered over 11 million in 1945, less than 4 million in 1946, and less than 2 million in 1947. Yet the decline in economic activity and the rise in the unemployment rate were short-lived. GNP (annual rates in current prices) fell from $224 billion in the second quarter of 1945 to about $198 billion in the first quarter of 1946. It then began to rise again. By the first quarter of 1947, it had regained its former peak level and continued to rise.

The employment situation was satisfactory. The unemployment rate did in fact rise sharply from its extremely low wartime level, but the 1945 and 1946 monthly rate averages were below 4 per cent. (In some particular months of the period, however, the rate was rather higher.)

The reconversion problem was slight for two important reasons. In the first place, new investment and export demands partially replaced defense demand very early, and state and local government purchases replaced it later. Secondly, consumption demand also increased, in spite of the fall in GNP. Personal disposable income—i.e., the money consumers had to spend after taxes—remained almost stable between the two quarters mentioned. This happened, in spite of unemployment, because of tax reductions and increased transfer payments, including unemployment insurance and veterans' allowances. These policies successfully prevented the GNP decline from becoming a decline in personal disposable income, which is one way in which initial declines in demand are transmitted to consumption and thus become cumulative. That, however, is not the whole story, for although personal disposable income remained stable, consumption actually increased greatly. Consumption not only did not aggravate the decline, it actually offset a major part of it.

Table 12 summarizes the change in GNP and its components between the second quarter of 1945 and the first quarter of 1946; quarterly amounts are multiplied by 4 to get an annual rate, and seasonally adjusted.

The offsets to the decline in defense spending arose partly from conscious policies and partly from exceptionally favorable circumstances. Lower tax rates and the increased transfers helped to support consumption as noted above (the budget still ran a small surplus for 1946 as a whole and larger ones in 1947 and 1948). Monetary policy was also definitely favorable to demand, as it kept interest rates low and credit access easy.

The exceptional circumstances were the tremendous liquidity and long pent-up needs of the economy. A large share of the war expenditures had been financed by borrowing, not taxation, and

Table 12

*Change in GNP and Its Components: Second Quarter 1945-
First Quarter 1946*

Demand Component	Peak-to-Trough Change (in billions of dollars)
Personal consumption	+18.5
Gross private domestic investment	+11.9
Net exports	+6.5
Government purchases	
National defense	−65.3
Other federal	+1.6
State and local	+1.1
Total	−25.7

Source: U.S. Department of Commerce, *U.S. Income and Output* (Washington, D.C.: USGPO, 1958), p. 120, and *National Income,* 1954 ed. (Washington, D.C.: USGPO, 1954), p. 224.

now consumers and investors began to spend their accumulated holdings of bonds. The long period of shortages, caused by the depression of the 1930s and the war, gave them urgent needs, and the liquidity gave them the means to satisfy these needs. Consumers were able to finance a large increase in consumption even though personal disposable income remained constant. In fact, consumption would probably have risen even without tax cuts.

The unemployment rate was also kept down by widespread withdrawal of workers, especially women, from the labor force and by a sizable reduction in working hours. These were natural responses to the elimination of the burden of the defense effort, because leisure had been curtailed in the war years. The total civilian labor force rose only about 4.5 million in 1946, much less than the nearly 8 million who left the Armed Forces. The average work week in manufacturing fell from 45.2 hours in 1944 to 40.3 in 1946. Because the discharge from the Armed Forces did not produce an equivalent increase in the supply of labor, the unemployment rate did not rise much.

These favorable circumstances would not be present in a future disarmament, assuming the initial situation was similar to the one that prevails now. There would probably be neither a desired decrease in the labor force nor a great supply of excess liquidity. There has not been a long period of unmet private needs. In the future, therefore, more extensive government fiscal policy would be needed. The private economy is unlikely to be buoyant enough to allow rapid recovery even with a budget surplus.

The conversion period was marred by inflation. Price controls were removed in 1946 and the Consumer Price Index, for example, rose 8 per cent in 1946 and 14 per cent in 1947. In fact, it was this rise in prices which helped keep the fall of GNP in current prices so slight. In constant prices or real terms, the decline in annual GNP from 1945 to 1946 was 14 per cent, compared to less than 2 per cent in current prices. And the 1945 real GNP had already fallen from the 1944 level. Measured in constant (1954) dollars, it was not until 1950 that GNP regained the 1944 level. This significant lag in the recovery of real GNP should not be counted against the success of reconversion, because wartime production levels represented unwelcome straining and temporary sacrifice of leisure. The unemployment rate is a better measure of success. And in 1946 the only component of real GNP which decreased was federal-government purchases; personal consumption did not. The point is only to demonstrate the great amount of inflation which took place and had positive evils of its own. This inflation arose more from changes in the demand mix than from an excessive aggregate level.[13] In other words, there was a shortage of capacity for a while in the production of specific goods, the demand for which was fed by the liquidity of consumers and investors. The very strength of that demand, however, rendered the aggregate conversion as easy as it was.

Such a sectoral inflation problem could occur after a future reduction in defense demand and its replacement by other demand, although the inflationary pressures would probably be much less. Disarmament would probably be more gradual, and defense production now constitutes a smaller part of total GNP. Neither would there be the great pressure for long-overdue adjustments in wages that characterized the post-World War II period. Nevertheless, some danger of inflation could be expected. Broad fiscal and monetary policies are inadequate to deal with the problem. Because prices and wages are usually flexible upward but rigid downward, a policy affecting only aggregate demand must keep the aggregate low enough to prevent inflation anywhere. This depresses demand far enough to cause intolerable unemployment in sectors where demand is already deficient—after disarmament, these would be the areas formerly dependent on defense. If localized inflation is a problem, finer and more discriminating policies are required to cope with it.

It is important to note the varying degree of success among sectors during the reconversion after World War II. Just as would be true in the future, the national average unemployment rate concealed significant variations. For example, the U.S. Department of Labor surveyed area unemployment rates in the spring of 1947, after the reconversion was well under way.[14] Some areas—including Tacoma, Portland-Vancouver, Sacramento, Stockton, San Jose, Los Angeles, San Bernadino, San Diego, Phoenix, Wichita, Mobile, and Tampa—still had unemployment rates of approximately 10 per cent. (The concentration of these areas on the Pacific Coast is noteworthy.) Other areas—such as Cleveland, Dayton, Hartford, Richmond, Milwaukee, and Indianapolis—had unemployment of less than 3 per cent.

In sum, the conversion problems were moderate in the aggregate, largely because of fortunate circumstances. These circumstances will probably not be present in the future, so more offsets to aggregate demand will have to be generated by monetary and fiscal policy than in 1945-46. The inflation and varying unemployment rates also provide important lessons, and are more representative of the problems that would be created by a future large reduction in defense production.

After Korea

A sharp reduction in defense purchases in 1953, after the end of fighting in Korea, clearly aggravated the 1953-54 recession, and in fact there is evidence that it caused the general decline.

The peak in GNP in current prices came in the second quarter of 1953; the trough, in the second quarter of 1954. The recession was rather brief and mild: GNP fell less than 3 per cent. The economy recovered and resumed growth in the last half of 1954. National defense purchases continued to decline, but slowly, while other components of demand rose by more than enough to offset this decline. The unemployment rate, however, remained well above 5 per cent for some time afterward.

The second quarter of 1953 was also the peak period for defense purchases. Obligations or orders for hard goods, however, had already dropped substantially in the latter part of 1952. In the last quarter of 1952 and the first two of 1953, the value of these obligations were much less than for the equivalent quarters of the previous year.

Table 13 shows again the changes between the peak and the trough. Federal purchases and inventory decumulation were the only large negative forces. The inventory reductions were partly caused by the decline in defense orders, and analysts also attach significance to a slowing in the growth in consumption before the decline started.[15] In the recession itself, consumption did decline slightly but had recovered before total GNP reached its trough, so a plus change is shown for consumption (see Table 13).

Table 13

Changes in GNP and Its Components:
Second Quarter 1953–Second Quarter 1954

Demand Component	Peak-to-Trough Change (in billions of dollars)
Personal consumption	+3.2
Gross private domestic investment	
Inventory change	−5.8
Other	0.0
Net exports	+1.5
Government purchases	
National defense	−9.0
Other federal	−2.8
State and local	+3.0
Total	−9.9

Source: U.S. Department of Commerce, *U.S. Income and Output* (Washington, D.C.: USGPO, 1958), pp. 120-121.

The recession could have been dampened, or perhaps even prevented, by more appropriate policy measures. This, of course, is much more obvious now, with the benefit of hindsight, than it was at the time. Federal nondefense purchases were reduced rather than expanded to cushion the impact. Before leaving office, President Truman had forecast a rapid fall in defense orders, but not in expenditures, during fiscal year 1954. In a concerted attack on the budget deficit, the new Eisenhower Administration hastened the decline in orders and expenditures, including those for nondefense items. The prospect of added declines became clear before the middle of 1953. By January 1954 the President could report that federal expenditures for fiscal year 1954 would run $7 billion less than planned by the preceding Administration.

Several opportunities for offsetting tax reductions were not used. The Korean War had brought tax-rate increases scheduled to expire soon: the corporation excess-profits tax on June 30, 1953; the individual income tax on December 31, 1953; the normal corporate-profits tax and certain excise taxes on March 31, 1954. Early in 1953 some suggested the possibility of earlier expirations. This was not favored by either Administration, because the economy was still in very high spirits. Eisenhower successfully advocated a six-month extension of the excess-profits tax and successfully opposed expiration of increases in individual income-tax rates six months before schedule. He unsuccessfully opposed the scheduled expiration of the increases in excise and corporate normal-profits taxes.

Had the expirations come earlier, the recession might have been less severe. As it was, they did provide a stabilizing force when they occurred. Monetary policy played a stronger role in providing offset demand—especially the strong residential construction increase in the upturn. The reductions in the Armed Forces were also carried out more slowly than they were after World War II.

It can be seen now that the favorable circumstances of the post-World War II reductions were not repeated, so a much smaller reduction had unfortunate effects. The experience shows that the private economy must be very buoyant indeed to withstand sharp reductions in defense demand without offsetting tax reductions and/or expenditure increases.

The 1957-58 Episode

A temporary reduction in defense demand played some role—but by no means the major role—in the recession of 1957-58. Declining export demand (after the unusually high levels of the Suez crisis) and a sharp drop in business investment—fixed and inventory—were the major initiators of the recession, but there were some added effects from a fall in defense contracts. The recession was short but deep and characterized by especially high unemployment rates.

From a $448.3 billion peak in the third quarter of 1957, GNP in current prices fell about 3.5 per cent to $432.9 billion in the first quarter of 1958. Given the continuing increase in the labor force, even such a small decline caused a large increase in unemployment. The unemployment rate began to rise in the second quarter of 1957 and reached a peak of 7.5 per cent (seasonally adjusted) in July and August 1958.

The defense demand showed up as a pronounced drop in defense orders, not in expenditures. Purchases for defense rose quarter after quarter, although at times slowly, through 1956 and the first three quarters of 1957. In the last quarter of 1957, the annual rate fell $1 billion, then began to rise again slowly. At no time during the recession did it vary more than $1 billion from $45 billion. The cut in new contracts was very large, however, and unfortunately it came at a time when the economy was weak; recession would probably have come sooner or later anyway, so the loss of defense demand merely removed a possible stabilizing force.

The drop in orders and its temporary nature is apparent from Table 14, which gives figures on obligations for hard-goods purchases, quarterly for 1956-58.

Table 14

Obligations for Hard-Goods Purchases: 1956-58
(in billions of dollars)

1956:1	4.5	1957:1	3.7	1958:1	4.8
:2	5.9	:2	3.4	:2	6.4
:3	3.9	:3	2.2	:3	2.6
:4	4.2	:4	4.0	:4	5.2
Total	18.5		13.3		19.0

Source: U.S. Joint Economic Committee, *Staff Report on Employment, Growth and Price Levels* (Washington, D.C.: USGPO, 1959), p. 285.

The reversal of the decline in obligations came quickly enough so that actual purchases remained almost stable. However, it prompted cutbacks in employment and inventory accumulations by contractors, adding to movements caused by declines in fixed investments and exports.

The cuts were especially severe for aircraft producers, as shown by their sharp reductions in employment. After a peak of 928,400 workers in April 1957, employment fell rapidly to 769,200 in May 1958 (a decline of nearly one sixth) before stabilizing and rising slowly again for awhile. The decline was somewhat greater for production workers than for nonproduction workers. In addition, the average weekly hours for production workers fell from 42.9 in December 1956 to 39.9 in November 1957.[16] Aircraft centers were among the first geographical areas to experience rising unemployment in 1957.

The military services introduced a number of other policies which hastened the reduction in inventory investment by contractors.[17] This was done in the hope of reducing expenditures quickly. On cost-reimbursement contracts, the U.S. Department of Defense adopted the policy of currently reimbursing only 80 per cent (instead of 100 per cent) of costs incurred, the remaining 20 per cent being paid only at delivery or as specified increments of work were completed. This increased the carrying costs of inventory and gave firms a very strong incentive to reduce such costs. On fixed-price contracts, the Department reduced the amount of progress payments made against work completed—from 75 per cent to 70 per cent on total costs and from 90 per cent to 85 per cent on direct labor and material costs alone.

The chief lesson to be learned from this episode is the importance of military contracts as new orders for certain industries. Predictions of the impact of changing defense expenditures must take these orders into account. In the event of future reductions, offsetting measures—if needed at all—will be needed before the budget shows falling expenditures. By that time the effects of reduced production and inventory reductions will have begun to cumulate.

Summary

In summing up past experience, we can re-emphasize these points:

1. Reductions in defense demand can depress the economy if they are not offset by private demand—either autonomous demand or demand arising from tax cuts and transfer increases—or by other government demand. The amount of offset to be initiated by federal policy will depend on the natural buoyancy of other sectors of the economy. Very favorable circumstances present after World War II will probably not be present in the future, so some direct offset programs will be necessary.

2. Even when defense resources were less specialized than they are now, a reduction in defense demand had varying effects on different industries and areas. The relative stability of employment and prices depends on the composition of the demand that replaces the defense demand and on the ease of transfer of resources.

3. The economic effects of a declining defense budget can be significantly felt before any decline in expenditures sets in, and adjustment policies must be ready to be applied as soon as orders begin to fall.

POLICIES TO COPE WITH DISARMAMENT

Proper public policies must be formulated to deal with the two major problems of disarmament: the general loss of demand caused by defense reductions; and the structural problem of matching the resources formerly devoted to defense to the new composition of demand.

The two problems are related and must be attacked simultaneously. If the new demand adequately replaces the old, but is one for which defense-industry resources cannot be adapted, these resources will remain unemployed. Inflation will result in sectors facing new demand but unable to expand capacity fast enough (assuming disarmament comes when there is little excess capacity). On the other hand, even nonspecialized resources will remain unemployed if there is no new demand of some kind to replace defense spending.

Appropriate public policy, therefore, must stimulate replacement demand and also help transfer defense resources into uses to satisfy the new demand. The latter policies can include influence on the composition of demand or assistance in the transfer—by retraining or relocation—of the resources.

Of course natural market forces in the economy will help to solve the structural problem by inducing the movement of resources. But even so, perfect solution to the structural problem is not possible. Some inflation will undoubtedly result from the shifts in demand, and some unemployment will persist for a time in localized pockets. The economy already contains, after all, such pockets ("depressed areas" are an extreme form), which are areas unable to adjust to changes in technology or demand. But policy goals should be set high. It is hoped that action will be rapid and determined enough to keep such structural maladjustments as few and as brief as is consistent with long-run reliance on the free market.

A successful policy for one problem will aid the solution of the other. High and growing general demand increases the natural mobility of resources; labor is more apt to move from industry to industry or area to area when there are prosperous industries and areas to which it can move. Natural obstacles to mobility—the reluctance to pull up roots, the fear of moving from bad to worse, the fear of being a stranger—can be partially lessened by prospects of full-time employment elsewhere. At the same time, specific policies to adapt resources to available demand—or to adapt demand to available resources—will reduce the danger of inflation for any given level of aggregate demand. Without specific structural policies, the movement of resources may come only after serious inflation in excess-demand areas has created large wage differentials.

We first discuss the aggregate problem alone, assuming there are no structural difficulties, i.e., that demand need only be maintained in the aggregate. Then we discuss the structural policies which seem advisable, taking care to point out what modifications are necessary in our earlier conclusions.

It should be noted that it is quite likely that disarmament will be slow and gradual, reducing the adjustment problems. The essay "Disarmament Assumptions" (Article 2), for example, projects—in line with the American position on a disarmament treaty—such a gradual decline. Many feel the problems will be no greater, in either the aggregate or the structural sense, than the normal ones raised each year by the continuing growth in capacity to be employed and by changes in technology. This may be true, but the addition of problems to problems cannot be ignored. Also, there is a rising standard for economic policy, so more will be expected of its makers. The real significance of gradual disarmament is that it will require, in larger measure, the same sorts of policies needed to cope with ordinary year-to-year problems.

General Demand-Offset Programs

To keep the unemployment rate from rising, every year the economy must generate an increase in demand sufficient to employ the added production capacity—a capacity increasing nearly 4 per cent per year because of growth in the labor force, net capital formation, and technological advance.[18] If defense spending declines, the economy must generate additional demand to replace the defense demand as well.

It is conceivable that no government policy changes would be necessary at all. Enough nonfederal demand (including state- and local-government purchases) may arise independently to insure full employment. This is conceivable, but not probable in the present kind of situation, for the economy has trouble maintaining full employment even with a stable defense budget. Few analysts seriously advocate no government action at all. For private demand independently to take up the slack would require increases in consumption, investment, net exports, or state- and local-government purchases. But except for state and local government, disarmament would have the likely effect of inducing declines in these components. Consumption might remain stable, because of the automatic stabilizers, but a significant rise in consumption would not be likely without tax cuts. A lack of growth in consumption would dampen investment, for new investment is induced by expected *growth* in demand. Exports would also probably suffer, for the reduction of defense expenditures abroad could reduce the earnings of foreign countries and their ability to buy from the United States. As for state- and local-government buying, its growth has in the past merely dampened falls in GNP, not prevented them.

We shall assume that some federal action is necessary if the conversion is to be rapid and is not to give rise to excessive unemployment. There are a number of actions possible, singly or in combination:

1. Reductions in federal tax rates.

2. Monetary policy to promote freer access to credit and lower interest rates.
3. Increases in federal purchases of nondefense goods and services.
4. Increases in federal transfer payments (that is, increases greater than the automatic increases resulting from unemployment in defense industries) to individuals or state and local governments.
5. Extension of more foreign aid to countries most likely to spend the dollars received on American exports. This would transform the "burden" of defense into the more satisfying burden of assistance to the poorer countries.

There are other actions possible, but these five would be the major possibilities. If disarmament really comes, it is probable that a combination of these will be used to broaden the attack on unemployment and to achieve certain other goals. The vital question however, is: What combination will be most effective?

Aggregate stability is not the only goal; other objectives will help to determine the particular policy mix. Because of extensive disagreement on these other goals, it seems imperative to hammer out rough decisions in advance, so that wrangling will not paralyze action when the need arises.

At the risk of oversimplification, we may discuss these other goals in terms of these questions:

1. What is the proper scope of government?
2. What is the proper scope of federal government relative to that of state and local government?
3. What is the proper income distribution?
4. What is the proper balance between investment and consumption?

These questions must be decided simultaneously, for the answer to one may affect the answers to others. For example, even if we decide to increase government expenditures, and not to cut taxes, we still must decide the distribution of the expenditures—by income class, by government level, and by investment versus consumption. The effects of transfer payments to the very poor will be different from those of federal spending on advanced civilian research. Both policies will keep federal activity large, but transfer payments will give rise to private consumption, while research is investment—and public investment at that. Also, transfer payments are likely to have an equalizing effect on income distribution, while the research programs probably will not.

It is clear, then, why a variety of programs will probably be used. The more variety there is, the more possible it will be to achieve balance—between investment and consumption; private and public goods; federal-, state-, and local-government goods. There remains the question of relative reliance. Although there can be more of both consumption and investment, for example, it is still true that the more consumption one gets, the less investment will be increased. Some combinations of goals, of course, may be impossible.

At any rate, a great many value judgments must be made. In addition, the choice of programs will also depend on the relative efficacy of each in stimulating demand. Some kinds of demand have more effect than others. Federal purchases of $1, for instance, cause directly a $1 increase in demand. A $1 increase in transfer payments may not, if part of that sum is saved and respent. This is not necessary, however; if the dollar goes to people who can then borrow on its strength, the spending effect may be higher. But if it does require more than a $1 transfer payment to induce a $1 increase in consumption demand, a larger deficit will have to be incurred per dollar of demand than with direct federal orders for goods. If there is some psychological or political limit to the deficit, there are reasons for favoring government purchases over transfer payments.

The impact of tax cuts, too, may be diminished by savings by the recipient. This is possible for both personal and for corporate tax cuts. The proportion of the latter which becomes aggregate demand, however, is more uncertain.

Consumers, as a group, are rather regular and dependable in their spending habits. Since World War II they have almost always spent 90 per cent or more of their disposable personal income. Even with a large and sudden change in income, as with the 1964 tax cut, this percentage was established after a short lag. But a firm will not necessarily use profits-tax reductions for investment. It may pass them on as dividends to stockholders, who are in general higher-income people and whose consumption fraction is somewhat lower than the average. The largest part, however, will probably

go at first into retained earnings reserves, not to dividends.[19] If
we were certain the funds would be invested in real capital goods,
the policy on corporate-tax cuts would depend on the preference
for investment versus consumption. But investment may not result.
The availability of funds aids investment only in a permissive way.
Firms will not invest every dollar of availabe funds if profit prospects are dim and there is already excess capacity. When tax cuts
are designed to offset reductions in defense demand, profits prospects may not be bright; the defense contractors will certainly be
gloomy, and their suppliers also. A corporate-tax cut alone, therefore, may not be effective. Investment may rise only after other demands put pressure on present capacity.

For these same reasons, sole reliance on monetary policy would
also not appear to be a wise strategy.[20] Many economists doubt that
the response in business investment to reductions in the interest
rate is strong, especially if there is excess capacity. (However,
easier credit would probably have some stimulating effect for
residential construction.) Strategically, it appears best to use some
corporate-tax reductions and to ease credit, but to set about increasing consumption and government demand as well in order
to complete the incentives for investment. In short, the preference
for a large increase in investment rather than in consumption or
government purchases may not be consistent with the aggregate
target for demand.

The analysis of tax cuts suggests that reduced defense demand
exactly matched by tax cuts will not result in the maintenance of
total demand, for some of the tax relief will not be spent on goods
and services. Taxes will have to be reduced more than purchases
to keep demand stable—the government will have to shoot for a
deficit (or, if there already is a deficit, an increase in it) right at
the start, unless there are independent rises in other components
of demand. Whether or not the deficit can be eliminated later depends on the strength of the economy.

On the other hand, declines in defense demand matched by
rises in other federal purchases—whether consumption or investment in nature—would require no increase in the deficit, for these
purchases automatically become demand. This is not a conclusive
argument for such an offset policy, because the relative demand
creation is not the only criterion of effectiveness.

We shall not multiply extensive examples here. The reader may find it interesting to analyze other possibilities—increased foreign aid, for example, or grants to state and local governments. In all cases the major considerations for a policy are its relative success in stimulating demand and its implications for other goals.

Structural Policies

We now turn to a discussion of the policies for structural problems. By *structural problems* we mean the difficulties of easy transfer of defense resources into other sectors—difficulties caused by physical and psychological obstacles to movement and the inadequate training of labor and experience of management.

One objective of such policies is to hasten the transition itself, provided that the resources are used efficiently in the new employment (meaning they are producing things more valuable than they would in alternative uses). Another objective is to prevent waste—even temporary waste—of resources which can make the transition only slowly. Prevention of waste is compatible with prevention of distress, because unemployment means distress and is also one manifestation of waste.

In a way, the achievement of the first objective assures achievement of the second. The faster the transfer out of old, outmoded lines of production into new ones, the shorter the period that resources will be kept idle. Nevertheless, there will be a minimum time required for transition. Any attempt to move resources too quickly may itself cause more distress. This minimum period may be quite long for some resources. The problem is to prevent waste of resources during this period while encouraging movement itself.

One approach is to do nothing positive—to leave the adjustment to market forces; in other words, to let decisions about the composition of demand (made by firms, consumers, and government budget-setters) proceed without regard for structural unemployment as long as aggregate offset is achieved. This approach would rely on market mechanisms to induce movement of resources from the defense-dependent regions and industries into those facing new demands. Owners who find their resources (including labor) unemployed will lower their asking price; workers will settle for lower wages and firms for lower profits. Owners who face strong demand will ask for higher wages and prices. The resulting price differentials will curb demand for the sought-after resources and shift it back to the idle resources. At the same time the differentials will induce movement of labor and capital into the greener pastures of higher wages and profits. Thus the needed transition is accomplished through the price mechanism.

It is true that the market will be of great assistance. This approach, however, contains flaws. First, there would be a lot of resistance to physical movement, because the populations in defense-dependent regions have roots and investments in housing and business. There is also resistance to accepting lower wages, even if the alternative is bleak; workers often remain idle rather than venture into new situations or accept low wages.[21] This resistance is broken down with time. Meanwhile, however, the resources are wasted. Increased unemployment insurance may reduce the hardship of the unemployed, but it is still true that there is waste for the whole economy.

The difficulty of movement from declining sectors is shown in the agricultural sector and in depressed areas. The market, in practice, works slowly and imperfectly. Large numbers of people remain in pockets of poverty while the nation in general enjoys economic prosperity.

The fact that many employees in defense—scientists and engineers, for example—are educated and mobile does not eliminate the problem. There is a secondary impact—on suppliers of raw materials and parts to final assemblers, and on local businesses which sell consumer goods to the employees more directly involved. The education and geographical mobility of workers in these firms may be much less.

A second problem is inflation. If transfers take time, and if total demand is maintained in the interim, there will be rising prices and wages in the sectors facing new demands. Inflation, of course, brings evils of its own. The complete hands-off approach, then, will cause additional distress. This is inevitable, because inflation in the booming sectors is the very mechanism by which resources are attracted and the desired movement accomplished. Because resources move only slowly, the inflation in the booming sectors may be substantial. And because prices in the declining sectors are very slow to move downward, the *average* level of prices also rises.

The success of the free-market approach will depend on the aggregate offset policies. The higher the general demand in the economy, the faster will the market forces operate. The opportunities for defense resources to transfer will be more favorable; Los Angeles aircraft workers will more easily find jobs in the Midwest automobile industry, for example, or in other industries in the Los Angeles area itself. It is also more likely, however, that there will be rapid rises in prices in the sectors responding to new demands.

Another approach to the adjustment problem goes to the other extreme. Under this approach, the government would guarantee employment for everyone by influencing the composition of demand. The government would tailor demand to suit the defense-dependent resources. A host of policies could be used: the government could fix the composition of its own purchases; it might increase civilian space expenditures merely to aid missiles and electronics firms; or it might finance more peaceful research in medicine, automated systems, and so on.

The government might also use discriminatory taxes and subsidies to channel demand. It might levy stiff excise taxes—or simply ration goods or credit—on items in excessive demand, and grant large subsidies to producers otherwise unable to compete in the open market. It might support the development of a supersonic air-transport fleet by making direct payments to airlines using such planes. It might grant tax relief to firms that have difficulty in adjusting to civilian markets, so that such firms could sell at lower prices and still make acceptable profits. And so on.

This approach has its justifications. Because disarmament is a national problem, perhaps the whole nation should bear the expense of preventing even short-run distress. There is the point that resources would otherwise be idle and produce nothing, and that getting them to produce something is better for all. The downward rigidity of prices and wages makes the resources "costly" to a private producer, even though there are no real costs at all to the economy as a whole. If the alternative is idleness, no real production is given up for the subsidized use—thus there is no real "opportunity cost." Private producers must use profit as a guide, so something must be done to make their use of the resources profitable. Direct government buying or subsidies are ways to do this. In the end, the whole economy produces more and uses more.

These arguments do justify some government intervention to facilitate movement and to support (for a time) resources which find adjustment difficult. But perpetual government support is not desirable. Short-run, temporary steps are appropriate, but long-run artificial support actually prevents market adjustments. The end result would only be production of things less valuable to the economy than would otherwise be demanded. The merit of such programs in supporting the affected groups would not outweigh the unwelcome composition of output. In short, the burden of national defense would be converted into another kind of burden.

Instead, structural policies for disarmament should facilitate natural market adjustments and, at the same time, support those people most seriously affected. If adjustment is possible, policy should provide pressure for it, along with support. Government assistance should be temporary, perhaps gradually declining over a period of a few years, and made conditional on efforts to find employment in sectors not requiring subsidy.

The form of the temporary government support will depend on a number of things, including tradition, past experience, and the degree of difficulty of adjustment for the firm or workers in question. General tax relief may be provided for firms seriously hurt by loss of defense demand. This would be tax reduction for specific companies, and would be in addition to any tax cuts used as a general aggregate demand policy. This policy would assist a firm during its conversion to, and initial operations in, some new line of production. These initial operations may not be very profitable because of the firm's lack of experience, but the lower tax rates will help to offset this disadvantage. If the firm actually runs a loss, however, profits-tax relief will not help, except insofar as a loss carryover reduces taxes on later profits. In such cases, direct subsidy payments may be necessary to keep the firm in business. These payments should be conditional only on continued operation, not on the production of particular goods or services. In other words, these payments should not be used to subsidize specific products. The choice of new product should be left to the firm, which will base its decisions on an analysis of the market. In the case of small firms, however, the government may finance expert analyses of the market and their own prospects in it.

Aid to firms is desirable because it lessens the adjustment burden on individual workers, especially their need to move. But because the support programs must be temporary, the new line of production must be profitable to the firm in the long run, even after the temporary tax relief ends. Some workers may not be suited to any industry appropriate for their geographical area, or they may not be suitable unless retrained. In these cases, public policy must use various retraining and relocation programs to aid their adjustment. Unemployment insurance should be increased, but in such a way as to make extended receipt of benefits conditional on participation in these programs. The programs could include expanded job-information and referral services, subsidization of moving expenses, perhaps compensation for losses in selling homes, and so on. Retraining, of course, already constitutes a large part of the government program to combat the problems of declining sectors and occupations.

Such a structural policy has many intricacies and administrative problems. Its successful implementation poses a challenge. The choice of firms to be given tax relief will be difficult, beyond the obvious cases. Policies to facilitate or force movement of labor will also be controversial. Choice among the many kinds of retraining programs involves some prediction of what skills will be useful in the future, and a significant choice must also be made between general education and more specialized training. Problems of physical movement over long distances will be troublesome. In this field, the services of social workers or other human-relations experts will be useful. They might aim at the movement of whole groups of families with previous ties, rather than single families, to lessen the problems of pulling up roots and putting them down again.

All these are merely examples. The process will not be an easy one, even given a generally high aggregate demand. But the more difficult and controversial the policies are, the more important it is that public discussion begin well in advance. Provisional agreements—expressing general commitment, but flexible in detail—should be outlined early. Perhaps the problems will turn out to be small, because of great mobility in the economy or because of the slow rate at which disarmament proceeds. But it is also true that the transitional delays we tolerate should then be shorter. Our standards of economic policy should be rather high, within the constraints of a generally free-market, private-enterprise economy.

Special Problems

There are a number of specific aspects of such a structural policy which should be discussed in more detail. First, there is the problem of inflation. Inflation resulting from sectoral shifts has been a problem before, even without a shift in defense expenditures.[22] As explained earlier, the shift in the composition of demand may cause net inflation. In the strong-demand sectors, this inflation may be the normal result of bidding up prices when supply cannot be increased fast enough. Or it may be caused by wage increases which exceed the increases in labor productivity (firms may then increase prices in an effort to maintain or increase profits). In any case, inflation can easily come before excessive unemployment is eliminated in all sectors.

The appropriate policies to deal with this kind of inflation are the subject of controversy, and whether or not the problem arises in connection with disarmament may make little difference. The current policy seems to be to use Presidential persuasion of labor and management to curb inflationary wage and profit-margin increases, while there has been little of the pressure on capacity that causes pure demand inflation in key sectors. The lack of such pressure comes from the continuing gap between actual employment and capacity. If there is a continued policy to eliminate the gap, the problems will presumably become more acute and persuasion may not be sufficient. The same applies to a postdisarmament situation, if fiscal and monetary policies aim at keeping a high level of general demand. If persuasion does prove insufficient, it may become necessary to use direct price, wage, or credit controls in order to reconcile the goals of price stability and full employment.[23]

Another hard question is: What is to be done if the adjustment of resources does not occur, even after several years? What should be done if the policies to induce transfer do not, in the end, succeed in certain cases? This could happen in the case of particular

occupational groups. More likely it will occur for certain geographical areas, and our discussion will be in those terms. The
government may find that, as the temporary-support period ends,
many people remain in an area which has been heavily affected by
defense cutbacks and which has not attracted new industry. Even
the best efforts may not be sufficient to encourage movement out
of the area, and there may be no prospects for the entrance of
permanent new industry without continuing support by the government.

This will not occur if an area has specialized in defense production before disarmament but has general advantages for other industry. The previous development will have built up an experienced
labor force, and caused the construction of housing and public
capital of the "social-overhead" type. Defense production may have
required the same transportation and communications links other
kinds of industry need as well. Some areas, then, will have a good
chance of attracting new industry. The temporary subsidy policies
may be useful, but not necessary in the long run; they will just
give a new firm—or new operations of old firms in the area—a
"cushion" for the initial period of unprofitable production. The
movement of labor and capital from one industry to another within
the area will be the only forced adjustment.

Other areas, however, may enter a long-run depression unless
given artificial support. They may have inadequate supplies of general capital and labor skills, having formerly been suited only to
some specialized defense operation. Or they may have some specific
shortcoming—such as lack of transportation access or insufficient
size to support efficient nondefensive production—shortcomings
which were no handicap for defense but are insurmountable for
other industry. What is the proper policy for such unfortunate
areas?

This problem would not be a new one. An area depressed by loss
of defense demand would be in the same boat as one hurt by loss
of textile manufacturing, timber resources, or ore deposits. The
problem is: How can the population be aided without too much
interference in the efficient allocation of resources?

If an area has literally no advantages except the labor and
physical capital left over from its more prosperous days, it may
be best not to grant continuing, long-run artificial support to in-

dustry there. Given a commitment to alleviate poverty, outright transfer payments to people are necessary. The resources "stuck" in the area will go to waste, and for quite a long time. But that may be preferable to artificial support inducing the creation of *new* resources (population growth and new capital) which would continue indefinitely to be wasted in inefficient production. With continued underutilization, the resources in excess supply will gradually disappear, through aging of the labor force and the wearing out of capital. The length of time required for attrition will only be lengthened by artificial employment opportunities. The outright support acceptable in these cases might be limited to those who cannot move at all, such as the aged. Of course, the administrative application of this rule is a difficult prospect.

Because this is a very hard choice to face, it is hoped there will be few or no areas of this kind, although it is best to face up to the possibility in advance. A brighter situation is presented by the area depressed because it lacks some key resource or advantage, such as a specific kind of capital, or transportation access. Here a public-investment or investment-subsidization program lasting longer than a few years may be required. A longer commitment to aid area redevelopment is consistent with economic efficiency if the productivity of the new capital is enhanced because the older, already existing capital complements the new. Redevelopment of older areas could be preferable to investment in new, empty areas as a way of meeting expanding population.

Finally, many defense resources overspecialized for private pro-duction may be efficiently employed in new or expanded public programs after disarmament. This does not mean the government may legitimately order missiles and airplanes merely to keep their producers busy. But there are desirable public programs to which defense resources would be especially suited. These programs are of the type not undertaken by private enterprise for profit, because the benefits are only to the society as a whole and cannot or should not be marketed, or because the risks are too great for private capital. They are government-financed civilian projects with the same characteristics as the weapons production now employing the resources. Just as defense is publicly financed because it is a public good, so other programs are public goods and could effi-ciently utilize the defense resources.

Rational calculation may call for the resources to be employed in this way—not because it is necessary for their continued employment, but because that is how they can *best* be used. Public programs can be expanded and initiated even if the resources have no problem finding other employment. These projects would be those which, before disarmament, had lower priority than defense and therefore had to be sacrificed but which, after disarmament, are of more value than any private production which used the resources.

Public opinion would probably support many such programs, so the government budget will not fall by the entire reduction in defense expenditures, even in the long run. A number of programs are discussed in the article by the U.S. Arms Control and Disarmament Agency (Article 3), along with opportunities for the private sector to absorb the capacity freed by disarmament. The choice of programs to be expanded will depend on the results of the budgetary process. Ideally, any expansion of the public sector should be based on a comparison of the costs and benefits relative to alternative utilization of resources to satisfy private demand.

Considerable expansion of the public sector seems inevitable even if calculations use the market prices of the resources as a measure of cost. Many feel the federal budget is now perpetually squeezed by the prior claim of defense. But the real or opportunity cost of resources is also an important factor. If the specialized, research-oriented resources now absorbed in defense encounter difficulty in adapting to civilian uses, they would temporarily go to waste unless used in very specific government programs. Certain public projects, therefore, would have a low *real* cost in the first years of operation, and this advantage might be enough to justify their long-run expansion. For example, assume that the benefits of civilian space exploration are felt to be less than those of public sewage-disposal plants of equal money cost. But only space programs can make use of certain facilities left over from the arms race, while the sewage-disposal plants require resources—construction labor, steel, cement, and the like—which have real alternative uses. The real cost of space exploration may be low enough to make its *net* benefit higher. In fact, careful calculations may justify extending space research beyond the period in which the leftover facilities would otherwise go to waste. However, there is a limit to the period over which space research could be carried on consistent with efficiency, if its benefits are actually less than those of sewage disposal. If the old facilities could have been adapted to other uses in three years, for example, a ten-year space program will have large real costs in its last seven years; a fifteen-year program, in its last twelve; and so on.

This is merely an illustration of the general principles involved, not an argument for more space research. After disarmament, the benefits of such research may be considered so small that they will not be worth even the low real costs assumed here. But the reader may think of other technologically advanced projects to which these principles would apply. He should bear in mind these principles when reading the statement by the Lockheed Aircraft Corporation (Article 6).

At any rate, consideration of the real costs of public projects must include an assessment of the alternative uses to which specialized labor and capital might be put. This consideration is one which ties together aggregate demand policy and structural policy. There really cannot be a decision on private versus public spending, and consumption versus investment spending, independent of decisions about what structural adjustments are necessary after disarmament. The shorter the time resources require for adjustment, the higher is their opportunity cost. In the long run, even very specialized resources have enough mobility to enjoy alternative opportunities, so no public project is justified unless it is of substantial benefit to society. The government cannot continue indefinitely to buy useless products from defense contractors merely to keep them in business, no matter how dismal the firms' prospects may appear at first glance.

CONCLUSION

The cost of one modern heavy bomber is this: a modern brick school in more than thirty cities. It is two electric power plants, each serving a town of 60,000 population. It is two fine, fully equipped hospitals. It is some fifty miles of concrete highway.[24]

This is the cost of defense: real goods and services we could produce with the resources now used for defense production. This is why defense is an economic burden. If disarmament comes, the burden can be reduced by transferring men and capital and technical skills into new uses. Disarmament is, therefore, a great goal. That defense also provides employment for millions of men should not prevent us from striving for this goal. We must, rather, plan ahead and agree on methods to insure the rapid transfer of resources to new uses after disarmament is achieved. Only then will the economic burden be lifted and the economic benefits of disarmament be realized.

Public policy need not do the entire job of smoothing and speeding adjustments, for the market will shoulder much of the task. But the market will work better in reallocating resources if there is a high level of aggregate demand. Even then there will be a need for policies which support temporarily the resources most affected, and at the same time let the market operate and even hasten the transfers it calls for.

Wide-scale disarmament should not be feared. It will be a boon, if we rise to its challenge. Neither should we fear the smaller, more gradual reductions in expenditures which are the result of new efficiency in producing defense. These reductions should also be welcomed; if we cannot eliminate the burden more quickly, every little bit of lightening helps. Even if the continuing reductions raise the same structural problems as wider-scale disarmament, this is no reason to oppose them. The problems can be solved, thereby providing valuable testing ground for the policies needed to cope with larger reductions in defense spending.

NOTES

1. Joint Economic Committee, *Impact of Military and Related Civilian Supply and Service Activities on the Economy* (Washington, D.C.: USGPO, 1964), p. 5.

2. "Our Defense Needs: The Long View," *Foreign Affairs* (April 1964), 366.

3. U.S. Senate Committee on Labor and Public Welfare, *Hearings, Nation's Manpower Revolution*, Part 7 (Washington, D.C.: USGPO, 1963), p. 2401.

4. U.S. Senate Committee on Labor and Public Welfare, *Convertibility of Space and Defense Resources to Civilian Needs: A Search for New Employment Potentials* (Washington, D.C.: USGPO, 1964), p. 619.

5. Joseph F. Fulton, "Employment Impact of Changing Defense Programs," *Monthly Labor Review* (May 1964), p. 510.

6. U.S. Department of Defense, *The Changing Patterns of Defense Procurement* (Washington, D.C.: Office of the Secretary of Defense, June 1962), p. 10.

7. Roger E. Bolton, *Defense Purchases and Regional Growth* (Washington, D.C.: The Brookings Institution, forthcoming). That study presents estimates for each state, but only the results for large regions are given here.

8. *Ibid.*

9. Donald F. Bradford, in U.S. Senate Committee on Labor and Public Welfare, *Hearings, op. cit.*, p. 2483.

10. The data in this section are from National Science Foundation, *Federal Funds for Research, Development, and Other Scientific Activities: Fiscal Years 1962, 1963, and 1964* (Washington, D.C.: USGPO, 1964); and *Reviews of Data on Research and Development,* No. 41, "Trends in Funds and Personnel for Research and Development, 1953-1962" (Washington, D.C.: USGPO, 1963).

11. General histories of this subject may be found in Bert Hickman, *Growth and Stability of the Postwar Economy* (Washington, D.C.: The Brookings Institution, 1960); Joint Economic Committee, *Staff Report on Employment, Growth, and Price Levels* (Washington, D.C.: USGPO, 1959), Chap. 8. The data in this section are from the *Staff Report,* various supplements to the U.S. Department of Commerce, *Survey of Current Business* (Washington, D.C.: USGPO), and *Economic Report of the President* (Washington, D.C.: USGPO, 1965).

12. Murray Weidenbaum, *Government Spending: Process and Measurement,* n. p., 1958.

13. Joint Economic Committee, *Staff Report on Employment, Growth and Price Levels, op. cit.*, p. 219.

14. U.S. Department of Labor, *The Labor Market* (Washington, D.C.: USGPO, May 1947 and June 1947), back cover.

15. Hickman, *op. cit.*, pp. 100-107.

16. U.S. Department of Labor, *Employment and Earnings Statistics for the United States, 1909-1964* (Washington, D.C.: USGPO, 1964), pp. 270-71.

17. Statement by Charles Hitch in Joint Economic Committee, *Hearings, Inventory Fluctuations and Economic Stabilization* (Washington, D.C.: USGPO, 1962), p. 114.

18. *Economic Report of the President, op. cit.*, p. 81.

19. Richard Musgrave, "Effects of Tax Policy on Private Capital Formation," in Commission on Money and Credit, *Fiscal and Debt Management Policies* (Englewood Cliffs, N. J.: Prentice-Hall, Inc.: 1963), p. 62.

20. Warren Smith, "Monetary and Fiscal Adjustments to Disarmament," in Emile Benoit and Kenneth Boulding (eds.), *Disarmament and the Economy* (New York: Harper & Row, Publishers, 1963).

21. John Dorsey, *The Mack Case: A Study in Unemployment,* unpublished doctoral thesis presented at Harvard University, Cambridge, Mass., 1963, discusses some of these mobility problems.

22. Charles Schultze, "Recent Inflation in the United States," Study Paper No. 1 of Joint Economic Committee, *Study of Employment, Growth, and Price Levels* (Washington, D.C.: USGPO, 1959).

23. *Economic Report of the President, op. cit.,* pp. 107-10, discusses some of these problems.

24. From a speech by President Eisenhower in 1953, quoted in Charles Hitch and Roland McKean, *The Economics of Defense in the Nuclear Age* (Cambridge, Mass.: Harvard University Press, 1961), p. 4.

PART I

The General Scope of Disarmament

BLUEPRINT FOR THE PEACE RACE

U.S. Arms Control and Disarmament Agency

On September 25, 1961, President Kennedy presented to the General Assembly of the United Nations the "United States Program for General and Complete Disarmament in a Peaceful World." On that occasion he used the phrase peace race. This program was elaborated in "Outline of Basic Provisions of a Treaty on General and Complete Disarmament in a Peaceful World," the American presentation to the eighteen-nation Committee on Disarmament meeting at Geneva. The proposals were for gradual disarmament, requiring more than six years. It seems probable that any disarmament treaty, though perhaps differing from the one outlined here, will call for such a gradual process. This will, of course, greatly lessen the economic-adjustment problems. The following is the summary of the Outline, reprinted from the U.S. Arms Control and Disarmament Agency's Blueprint for the Peace Race (May 1962).

PRINCIPLES AND PROCESS OF DISARMAMENT

Disarmament would be implemented progressively and in a balanced manner so that at no stage could any State or group of States obtain military advantage. Compliance with obligations would be effectively verified. As national armaments were reduced, the United Nations would be progressively strengthened.

Disarmament would be accomplished in three stages—the first to be carried out in three years; the second, also in three years; and the third, as promptly as possible within an agreed period of time. Stage I would be initiated by the United States, the Soviet Union, and other agreed States. All militarily significant States would participate in Stage II; and all States possessing armaments and armed forces, in Stage III.

Transition from one stage of disarmament to the next would take place upon a determination that all undertakings in the preceding stage had been carried out and that all preparations for the next stage had been made.

DISARMAMENT MEASURES

A. ARMAMENTS

During Stage I, inventories of major categories of both nuclear delivery vehicles and conventional armaments would be reduced by 30 per cent. Fixed launching pads would be reduced with associated missiles. Half of the remaining inventories would be eliminated during Stage II, and final reductions would be made in Stage III. Upon the completion of Stage III, States would have at their disposal only agreed types of nonnuclear armaments for forces required to maintain internal order and protect the personal security of citizens.

Production of armaments during Stage I would be limited to agreed allowances and would be compensated for by the destruction of additional armaments to the end that reductions would not be impaired. In Stage II, production of armaments would be halted except for parts for maintenance of retained armaments. Any further production of national armaments would be ended in Stage III except for production of agreed types of nonnuclear armaments for internal forces.

Military research, development, and testing would be subject to increasing limitations during the disarmament process. During Stage III, appropriate action would be taken to insure that new scientific discoveries and technological inventions of military significance were not used for military purposes.

B. ARMED FORCES

Force levels of the United States and Soviet Union would be reduced to 2.1 million at the end of Stage I. Half of the remaining forces of these two States would be disbanded during Stage II, and final reductions would be made in Stage III. Other States would also progressively reduce their force levels. By the end of Stage III, States would have at their disposal only those agreed forces and related organizational arrangements required to maintain internal order and protect the personal security of citizens.

C. NUCLEAR WEAPONS

Production of fissionable materials for use in nuclear weapons would be halted in Stage I, and limitations would be imposed on the production of fissionable materials for other purposes. The availability of fissionable materials for use in nuclear weapons would be reduced during Stage I and subsequent stages by safeguarded transfers to nonnuclear weapons purposes.

If nuclear-weapons tests had not already been halted under effective international control, arrangements to this end would be undertaken in Stage I. States which had manufactured nuclear weapons would agree in Stage I not to transfer control over nuclear weapons to States which had not manufactured them or to assist such States in their manufacture. States which had not manufactured nuclear weapons would refrain from seeking them. Transfers of fissionable materials between States would be limited to peaceful purposes and would be safeguarded.

Beginning in Stage II, nonnuclear components and assemblies of nuclear weapons would be destroyed and limitations would be imposed on further production or refabrication of nuclear weapons. At the end of Stage II, remaining nuclear weapons would be registered internationally to assist in verifying the fact that by the end of Stage III States would not have such weapons at their disposal.

D. OUTER SPACE

The placing of weapons of mass destruction in orbit would be prohibited in Stage I, and limitations would be imposed on the production, stockpiling, and testing of boosters for space vehicles. States would support increased cooperation in peaceful uses of outer space.

E. MILITARY BASES

Reduction of military bases, wherever they might be located, would be initiated in Stage II, and final reductions would be made in Stage III.

F. MILITARY EXPENDITURES

Military expenditures would be reported throughout the disarmament process.

VERIFICATION

The verification of disarmament would be the responsibility of an International Disarmament Organization, which would be established within the framework of the United Nations. Reductions of armaments and armed forces would be verified at agreed locations; and limitations on production, testing, and other specified activities, at declared locations. Assurance that agreed levels of armaments and armed forces were not exceeded and that activities subject to limitation or prohibition were not being conducted clandestinely would be provided through arrangements which would relate the extent of inspection at any time to the amount of disarmament being undertaken and to the risk to the disarming States of possible violations.

Such assurance might, for example, be accomplished through arrangements under which States would divide themselves into a number of zones through which inspection would be progressively extended. By the end of Stage III, when disarmament had been completed, all parts of the territory of States would have been inspected.

REDUCTION OF THE RISK OF WAR

To promote confidence and reduce the risk of war during the disarmament process, States would—beginning in Stage I—give advance notification of major military movements and maneuvers, establish observation posts to report on concentrations and movements of military forces, and insure rapid and reliable communications among heads of governments and with the Secretary-General of the United Nations.

An International Commission on Reduction of the Risk of War would examine possible extensions and improvements of such measures as well as additional measures to reduce the risk of war through accident, miscalculation, failure of communications, or surprise attack.

ARRANGEMENTS FOR KEEPING THE PEACE

In Stage I, States would undertake obligations to refrain from the threat or use of force of any type contrary to the United Nations Charter. Throughout the three stages of disarmament, States would use all available means for the peaceful settlement of disputes, would seek to improve processes for this purpose, and would support measures to improve the capability of the United Nations to maintain international peace and security.

A United Nations Peace Observation Corps would be established in Stage I, and a United Nations Peace Force, in Stage II. The United Nations Peace Force, which would be equipped with agreed types of armaments and would be supplied agreed manpower by States, would be progressively strengthened until, in Stage III, it would be fully capable of insuring international security in a disarmed world.

DISARMAMENT ASSUMPTIONS

Panel on Economic Impacts of Disarmament

In 1961 a panel of experts prepared a report on the economic impacts of disarmament for the U.S. Arms Control and Disarmament Agency. In the part of the report reprinted here, the panel translated American disarmament proposals (see the preceding article 1) into estimated changes in military and related spending. The figures are only estimates, of course, and do not represent firm expenditure decisions by the government. It should be noted that defense expenditures fell slightly in 1964 even without a treaty, so a treaty might bring about an even more rapid decline than the one projected here. The members of the panel were Emile Benoit, Chairman; Blanche Bernstein, Prentice N. Dean, Marvin Hoffenberg, Richard R. Nelson, Robert M. Solow, Robert Steadman, Murray Weidenbaum, and Nat Weinberg. The full report is contained in the U.S. Arms Control and Disarmament Agency's Economic Impact of Disarmament *(January 1962).*

In attempting to project the economic impact of disarmament, it is first of all necessary to have a reasonably clear-cut set of assumptions about the nature and timing of the disarmament process. . . . [Although] these matters are and will continue to be the subject of negotiation, the ultimate outcome of which can hardly be predicted at this stage, it is nonetheless necessary to make assumptions about the general character of the disarmament process with respect at least to those factors that will have a decided economic impact.

The disarmament assumptions we used in making our projections are intended to be generally consistent with the major U.S. disarmament objectives and policies as set forth in the proposals presented by . . . President [Kennedy] to the United Nations. The model was, however, designed by the panel. The timing and phasing of disarmament used in the model are, in the judgment of the panel, the optimum that can realistically be expected from the negotiation and implementation of general and complete disarmament in view of the fundamental and complex factors involved and in view of the negotiating history of recent years. However, the specific measures and dates assumed in the model involve matters upon which determinations of U.S. policy have not yet been made.

With a different concept or model of disarmament, the economic implications might be considerably altered. For example, an arms-control agreement involving a major change in the weapons mix might involve no reduction in defense expenditure and, because of the heavy new inspection costs, might even make for some net increase in military budgets—at least for a time. Similarly, a crash disarmament program, such as might arise out of a crisis situation described by T. C. Schelling under the heading "Reciprocal Fear of Surprise Attack," or a region-by-region sequential disarmament pattern as suggested by Louis Sohn, would considerably change the economic impact. Such more remote alternatives have been ignored here, to concentrate on the possible implications of more conventional conceptions of disarmament.

Even within such a conception, some of the elements are economically more strategic than others. Any important changes made with respect to these elements during the course of negotiation of a disarmament agreement could, in some degree, undermine the projections and analyses of this report.

One crucial assumption in this sense is with respect to the date of the cutoff in new production of delivery vehicles and nuclear warheads. Another is the pace of demobilization of personnel. Another is the magnitude and type of inspection, police, and deterrent forces established under an international control organization (or, as the September 25th plan calls it, IDO—International Disarmament Organization) and responsible for administering and enforcing the disarmament agreement. The rate and timing of the buildup of such forces is likewise very important. (It should be noted that the cost of the inspection service is a particularly uncertain item, with a very wide dispersion of estimates among experts with respect to the type and amount of inspection activities and equipment and even with respect to the probable costs of particular inspection systems.) Another assumption of obvious importance is with respect to the total duration of the disarmament program. Finally, the projected severity of the disarmament impact will also be affected by the assumptions with respect to the size of the national forces at the beginning of the program and after disarmament is completed.

Our model is in line with informal estimates of 1965 defense expenditures as falling within the range of $50-$60 billion. We have used the upper end of this range in order to reduce the likelihood that our projections of disarmament impacts would underestimate the extent of the problem. With respect to other economically strategic assumptions mentioned above, we have sought to choose those assumptions which seem most in line with the official disarmament proposal and have checked the quantitative estimates with the opinion of experts wherever possible—adopting compromise figures wherever the range of expert opinion was itself very wide.

The disarmament model adopted by the panel for the purposes of this report, and its implications for U.S. security expenditures—national and international—are shown in Table 1. In approximate terms, it projects a decline in defense expenditure of $17 billion (1960 dollars) in the first three years, a further decline in national defense programs in the second stage of $12 billion partly offset by a $3.5 billion contribution to international inspection costs, and so forth (i.e., a net reduction of about $8.5 billion), and a further net reduction in the third (two-phase) stage of $13.5 billion in the last six years. The total net reduction in U.S. security expenditures (after allowance for the U.S. contribution to the costs of an international organization responsible for inspection, police, and deterrent functions) would thus be about $38.5 billion over a twelve-year period, with roughly $6 billion a year in the initial three-year period.

These cutbacks might be partly offset by a buildup in certain programs which have been closely associated with our defense effort in the past, such as NASA [National Aeronautics and Space Administration] and the civilian AEC [Atomic Energy Commission] programs. The projections with respect to these programs shown in Table 1 include an allowance for the NASA moon program re-

Table 1

Model of General and Complete Disarmament
U.S. Expenditures for Security and Associated Programs*
(in billions of 1960 dollars)

	1960	1965	Stage I 1965-68	Stage II 1968-71	Stage IIIA 1971-74	Stage IIIB 1974-77
U.S. Defense**						
Personnel	11.7	15.1	13.1	11.1	6.7	4.7
Operation and maintenance	10.2	12.6	8.9	6.0	3.9	2.1
Procurement (including research and development)	18.0	20.9	12.2	6.3	4.8	1.5
Other	5.3	7.5	4.7	3.6	1.9	1.9
U.S. defense total†	45.2	56.1	38.9	27.0	17.3	10.2
U.S. contribution to international forces††	...	...	...	3.7	4.9	7.1
Total U.S. expenditures on security programs	45.2	56.1	38.9	30.7	22.2	17.3
Associated programs						
NASA	0.4	2.7	4.5	5.9	7.4	8.9
Civilian AEC	0.5	1.4	2.0	2.0	2.0	2.0
Total	46.1	60.2	45.4	38.6	31.6	28.2

* Disarmament assumptions are intended to be broadly consistent with the U.S. program.

** Defense expenditure estimates made by READ [Research Program on Economic Adjustments to Disarmament] based on U.S. Bureau of the Budget projections, published in *Special Study* (January 1961); George Steiner's unpublished manuscript, "Defense Activities in Southern California in the 1960s"; and confidential industry sources.

† Excluding revolving fund.

†† The U.S. contribution to the international control organization and the Peace Force is assumed to cover one third of total costs, but no charge is assumed for existing weapons or bases transferred to the international control organization or the Peace Force.

cently announced, and so on. If the revised projections prove realistic, the offsets provided by the expansion of both "associated programs" . . . would be close to a total of $2.5 billion over the initial
three-year period of maximum defense cutbacks. The total expansion of these programs over the whole disarmament program is
estimated at $6.8 billion, based on existing plans. If these programs
are accelerated between . . . [1961] and 1965, this could result in
a slower pace of buildup between 1965 and 1977 than assumed in
our model but would more likely be associated with a corresponding increase in the size of the 1977 program so that the projected
increase between 1965 and 1977 might not be greatly changed. Our
projections, incidentally, do not involve additional space programs
which might be adopted as specific disarmament offsets.

If we take account of the offset provided by the costs of inspection forces and the buildup of the NASA and civilian AEC programs,
we find a net reduction in U.S. security and associated expenditures of about $22 billion in the first six years, with only about $5
billion a year during the crucial introductory three-year period of
maximum impact.

PART II

Economic Implications of Large
Defense Reductions

THE ECONOMIC AND SOCIAL CONSEQUENCES
OF DISARMAMENT

U.S. Arms Control and Disarmament Agency

In 1961 the United Nations asked a Consultative Group of Experts, appointed by the Secretary-General and representing various nations, to examine the worldwide aspects of disarmament. The group's report recommended that governments of countries bearing a major share of the world's arms burden submit further studies of their own countries. The U.S. Arms Control and Disarmament Agency's response to this recommendation was a report submitted to the Secretary-General in 1962. The following are excerpts from this study, entitled The Economic and Social Consequences of Disarmament, *as revised in 1964. Many issues not discussed in these excerpts are examined elsewhere in the study.*

INTRODUCTION

The motivating force behind the efforts of the United States to achieve general and complete disarmament under effective international control is to save present and future generations from the scourge of war and to attain for them a more certain and beneficent security.

This basic and vital objective completely overshadows any economic calculations of gain or loss connected with disarmament. Actually, the United States can maintain as high or as low a level of defense expenditures as is deemed necessary for its security. At the same time it is clear that a basic change in our methods of achieving security will have distinct effects on our economy. Any examination of the question of disarmament therefore requires study of its economic impact in order to enlarge our understanding of the policies, programs, and actions required to derive the maximum economic and social benefit from it for ourselves and the rest of mankind.

It must be stressed that the allocation of resources to purely military purposes is not an economically creative process, except in an incidental way. It yields relatively few goods or services which contribute to the enrichment of individual lives or to the growth of the national economy. It prevents or retards the satisfaction of many civilian needs. By the same token, if the world should be fortunate enough to the able to rid itself of the burden of national defense efforts, resources would then be released everywhere which could be devoted to the production of those goods and services which advance man's material, cultural, and spiritual state. This is the basic economic interest of the United States in disarmament, and it is an entirely positive one.

This study of the extent to which the defense effort affects the American economy, and of the economic problems and opportunities which would be encountered under a program of general and complete disarmament, is in no sense definitive. This is because there are important gaps in our basic knowledge of detailed facts and because there is as yet no indication as to the timing, phasing, and duration of the disarmament program which may eventually emerge from international negotiations.

Despite these limitations, it is possible to arrive at several significant conclusions.

1. The current national defense effort of the United States takes about one tenth of our . . . [GNP] and employs somewhat less than that portion of our employed labor force. . . . As a component of total economic demand, defense expenditures are not of such magnitude that the economy is vitally dependent on them. In fact, the American economy proved itself after World War II to be very resilient to a considerably greater and more rapid reduction in defense expenditure than would be involved under any disarmament program starting at the present level of armaments.

2. The currently recognized needs of Americans individually and

collectively are so extensive that, if translated into economic demand, they would more than offset the loss of demand resulting from an agreed disarmament program. . . .

3. Unquestionably, any program of disarmament will in the short and intermediate run give rise to problems of adjustment in all factors of production. However, these adjustment problems—of varying intensity depending on the timing, phasing, and duration of any agreed disarmament program—are not novel to the America economy; quite apart from previous successful adjustments to major changes in defense expenditures, the economy is constantly undergoing adjustment in a wide range of industries as a result of changes in technology and economic demand. Concerted effort on the part of government at all levels and of business and labor, to bring to bear numerous available instruments and, if necessary, to create additional ones, can reduce to a minimum any hardship and waste in the adjustment process under a program for general and complete disarmament.

4. The United States has long recognized that general and complete disarmament would present opportunities for enlarged assistance to less developed countries and has sponsored United Nations resolutions in this sense. . . . When and as disarmament is achieved, the American people can be expected to face imaginatively the added challenges and opportunities which this development would hold for the welfare of mankind.

5. In the area of international economic relations, the elimination . . . of U.S. government defense-related expenditures abroad, and of defense-related imports, . . . would have a corrective effect on the U.S. balance-of-payments deficit. There would probably be a noticeably adverse effect in only a few countries; these effects could be overcome with increased external economic assistance and growth and diversification in the respective economies. The elimination of military-oriented production and trade controls under disarmament would permit more international trade to flow on the basis of comparative advantage.

THE PROBLEMS OF ADJUSTMENT TO DISARMAMENT

In considering the problems which must be dealt with if, as, and when an agreed disarmament program permits the American people to reallocate the human and material resources now devoted to defense, two important factors must be taken into account.

CONTINUING EXPENDITURES FOR SECURITY

In the first place, it is clear that, even in a disarmed or disarming world, resources—possibly substantial ones—must be devoted to the maintenance of security. In this connection it is useful to recall the Joint U.S.-U.S.S.R. Statement of Agreed Principles for Disarmament Negotiations, of September 20, 1961:

. . . During and after the implementation of the program of general and complete disarmament, there should be taken, in accordance with the principles of the United Nations Charter, the necessary measures to maintain international peace and security, including the obligation of States to place at the disposal of the United Nations agreed manpower necessary for an international peace force to be equipped with agreed types of armaments. . . .

. . . The logical conclusion from the foregoing is that the achievement of "general and complete disarmament" . . . will not relieve the United States and other nations of the necessity to continue to allocate . . . resources for . . . international peacekeeping. Indeed, the new forms and instruments of security will have first call on . . . resources which would be released by the elimination of our national military program. To the—at this time unknown— extent that this occurs, it would naturally reduce somewhat the scope of the over-all conversion problem.

TIMING, PHASING, AND DURATION OF DISARMAMENT

The second consideration affecting examination of the economic effects of disarmament is that at this time there is no indication when a disarmament agreement might go into effect, how its incidence on particular defense expenditures would be phased, and how long it would be before the entire process has been concluded. Yet these variable factors have profound effect on the problems of economic adjustment. . . .

In the absence of specific details on the timing, phasing, and duration of a disarmament program, it is therefore not possible to discuss the problems of adjustment except in general terms.

TWO BASIC PROBLEMS OF ADJUSTMENT

It is important to distinguish between two basic problems of adjustment. The first is to maintain aggregrate economic demand in the nation despite more or less substantial and progressive declines in demand from the defense sector. The second is to minimize hardships and waste as the human and material resources now devoted to defense find new uses.

These two problems, . . . [although] different in nature and in the policy instruments suited to deal with them, are interconnected. Thus, if there is general inadequacy of aggregate demand, it will be more difficult, if not impossible, to overcome the structural problems of transition. On the other hand, if the transition from national defense efforts to general and complete disarmament should be characterized by persistent structural maladjustment, the effect of measures to maintain aggregate demand on output and employment would tend to be dissipated in inflation. With advance planning and sensible policies at all levels of government and on the part of business and labor, it should be possible to master both of these problems satisfactorily.

Maintaining Aggregate Demand

It is clear that, if not offset, significant and progressive declines in defense spending would reduce the growth rate of economic activity and quite possibly bring about an absolute decline. In the absence of compensating factors, total demand would be reduced by significantly more than the reduction in defense spending. Declining defense spending would be reflected in reduced income for employees of the defense industries and of the industries supplying, directly and indirectly, the defense contractors. Decreases in personal income would be moderated, to some extent automatically, by reduced taxes and increased transfer payments; but, with existing legislation, a . . . [$1] reduction in defense spending would cause, directly and indirectly, about a . . . [$1] reduction in personal consumption. In addition, the decline in aggregate demand would lead to a reduction in capacity and inventory requirements and thus to some fall in the rate of investment.

In the event of disarmament it would be necessary to encourage, stimulate, or create those offsets which would counteract these negative factors to the maximum extent and absorb the slack in the economy. The nature of the required policies is well understood, and historical experience testifies to the ability of the American economy to respond in a healthy way to major reductions in defense expenditures. . . .

MEETING THE PROBLEM OF AGGREGATE DEMAND

The most important factor to bear in mind in meeting the problem of aggregate demand . . . is that . . . there are in the United States as well as in other countries very substantial unmet needs and opportunities which could work as a powerful factor on the economy. . . . Some of these needs and opportunities will be described in greater detail in the next . . . [section]. Many of them will be increasingly met as the decade progresses, whether there is a program for general and complete disarmament or not, but they will not be eliminated; moreover, new needs will become apparent with the passage of time.

Reference has been made to the role of dynamic optimism in our society after World War II as a positive influence on economic development. It would be hard to imagine that the American people would not respond very positively to an agreed and safeguarded program to substitute an international rule of law and order for the present national security efforts, once the full implications of such a change were understood. The beneficent effect of such a development on the economic plans and actions of the American people, acting individually and through their institutions, would be incalculable.

Even without the psychological stimulus that could be expected from the type of disarmament program which it is the object of our policy to obtain, the American economy does not lack dynamism. It is the strength of the free-enterprise system that it not only affords large opportunities for the exercise of inventive genius and economic initiative but, in fact, inspires them on a large scale. These are among the principal forces which have provided the motive power for the growth of the American economy, and they will certainly contribute significantly to maintaining the momentum of the economy in the event of disarmament.

Government policy will have a vital role in dealing with the problem of aggregate demand. Sensitive response to the particular economic facts and forces prevailing prior to and at the commencement of disarmament and far-sighted action can contribute strongly to the creation of the conditions which will allow the unmet needs of society to be translated into the kind of economic demand that will—potentially—more than take up the slack caused by the progressive decline in national defense spending. Several powerful tools and instruments are available to the federal government and, to a more limited extent, to state and local governments, for this purpose. . . .

All these tools were used successfully after World War II and some after the Korean War. There is no reason why they should not be used, with maximum impact, again. In this connection it is of interest to note the President's recent request to Congress for standby authority to accelerate public improvement programs, to implement income-tax reductions, and to provide extended unemployment-compensation payments in the event of threatening recession. Adoption of this proposal would, of course, be most helpful in dealing with substantial declines in defense spending under a disarmament program.

Determination of the precise combination of measures to support aggregate demand under a disarmament program is in itself a complex process requiring advance planning, continuing evaluation of economic developments and likely economic impacts, and political decision. As noted at the beginning of this . . . [section], the success of any program of maintaining demand will also be dependent on the success of parallel measures to deal with any structural problems such as regional or local concentration of defense activities, and industry and manpower specialization.

At every step there will be the problem of making choices, of striking the most appropriate balance between numerous possible courses of action, each of which will have a different impact on the economy. Thus, either an increase in government expenditures for goods and services or a decrease in taxes increases aggregate demand and brings additional resources into employment. Either action has a multiplier effect which is greater than its initial impact. . . . Thus, either tax reduction or increased government spending indirectly stimulates almost all categories of private demand, and, in particular, private consumption. But the direct effect of a tax reduction is to employ resources for private consumption or investment, while the direct effect of government spending is to employ resources on production of public goods and services.

The proper balance between tax reduction and increased public civilian expenditures will involve an economic and political evaluaiton of the relative priorities of the goods and services which would be purchased by households and businesses if their incomes were greater . . . as against those of public goods. . . . Similarly. the proper balance between reduced personal and excise taxes on the one hand and reduced profits taxes, and a policy of easy money on the other will be governed, generally, by the relative importance accorded respectively to consumption and investment.

An element of uncertainty . . . would be the precise reaction of private consumption, and of private investment in plant and equipment and inventories, to the decline in defense orders and to the compensating policies. . . . However, the very fact that the timing, phasing, and likely duration of a disarmament program would be known well in advance to policy-makers places the whole problem . . . on a considerably more certain and favorable basis than is normally available for the development of countercyclical policy. Utilization of this favorable circumstance . . . to prepare in advance the desirable offsetting measures . . . would have a most beneficial effect on public confidence that the economic and social benefits of disarmament would be realized. This in itself would be a potent factor, making for success in the adjustment process.

Overcoming Structural Problems

THE PROBLEM

Any considerable change in the composition of final demand is bound to require some degree of structural adjustment as regards both manpower and physical facilities, and it may entail geographic redistribution of production and related activities. Actually the economy is constantly experiencing structural changes as a result of technological developments, the introduction of new products and services, population developments, and other factors. Taken together, these changes over a period of time are substantial, and . . . [although] it cannot be said that they have always proceeded with a minimum of hardship and waste, nevertheless, it is clear that they have not prevented the attainment of substantial growth in the economy.

Disarmament could, and probably would, seriously add to the problems of structural adjustment. . . .

. . . One of the principal characteristics of the current defense effort is the relatively high concentration of its economic impact geographically and by industry. Moreover, a large share of defense work is in the hands of specialized defense contractors whose product and expertise may not be readily adaptable to production for a civilian market. . . .

Under the circumstances disarmament will require some shifting of manpower to new industries, occupations, and possibly even to new locations. Many plants will have to convert to new lines of production, and to the extent that such conversion on existing sites is not possible or desirable, relocations, and, in some cases, liquidations may be in order; also, it is to be expected that new industries will have to be encouraged to establish themselves in many areas where defense production is now concentrated.

These structural adjustments would be faced in the context of the sizable increase in the labor force and in automation which is expected to develop over the coming years.

It will be desirable to bend every effort to reduce the friction in the process of adjustment to a minimum, in order to minimize hardship and waste, and as another means of maximizing the benefits of disarmament. There are several significant instruments and factors as well as a growing body of experience which will be helpful in this connection.

AREA REDEVELOPMENT

Increasing attention has been given by government, labor, and business to the problem of depressed areas, which is directly relevant to the problem of adjusting to disarmament because of the heavy geographic concentration of the defense effort. . . .

Recognition that redevelopment of "depressed areas" which already exist in our country was a matter transcending local interest led to the adoption of the Federal Area Redevelopment Act, under which the federal government seeks to assist local and state groups in the economic development of areas with high and persistent unemployment. . . . One of the principal achievements of this new legislation has been the encouragement of hundreds of communities to develop over-all economic development plans. These communities are thus better able to cope with any kind of economic adjustment that may be necessary—whether it be . . . [the result of] armament cutbacks, trade impacts, automation, depletion of natural resources, or other causes.

The deactivation of defense installations in the course of a disarmament program will create specific redevelopment situations. . . . It will no doubt be found that many of these facilities can be adapted to civilian uses in such fields as education, health, research, recreation, and industry. Such adaptation will benefit from adequate and coordinated advance planning by the local communities, the federal government, and other interested elements; it could make a real contribution not only to the life of the affected communities but also in filling some of the over-all needs for plant and equipment which are discussed [later]. . . .

. . . The practical lessons under the Area Redevelopment Act and the numerous other measures and programs having the same general objective will be invaluable in dealing with such significant local or regional dislocations as may be caused by disarmament.

INDUSTRIAL CONVERSION

In our free-enterprise system the task of converting industrial production from defense to civilian uses will in the main rest on the affected firms, responding to the actual and anticipated demands in the market at home and abroad. . . . The problems will not be basically different from those which continually arise in a changing economy. The increasing emphasis which many American firms place on careful analysis of trends and prospects . . . in . . . markets . . . will be most helpful in meeting the conversion problem. . . . Many firms will no doubt . . . accelerate their civilian . . .

research and development, in some cases readily reallocating facilities and manpower now devoted . . . to military work.

Policies and measures which the federal government will apply to the termination . . . of defense contracts under progressive disarmament . . . could be designed with a view to facilitating the adjustment process in the affected firms. There is a considerable body of successful experience in this area in connection with the demobilization at the end of World War II. The federal government could also aid the adjustment process by extending loans and technical assistance to those firms which have a particular need for such support. . . .

ADAPTABILITY OF AMERICAN LABOR

The mobility of the American labor force is one of the nation's assets in adjusting to economic change. This is true whether the need for change arises out of the development of new industrial technology and shifts in civilian demand or whether it is induced by mobilization or disarmament.

Geographically, there has been continuous movement from one area to another in the United States. Many of these moves are to nearby areas, but others are long moves between states. . . .

Many American workers also move into and out of the labor force by choice. During the course of a single year the . . . labor force varies by several million from the seasonal peak in the autumn to the low . . . in the late winter. Most adult men over twenty-five and under sixty-five who are able to work are permanently attached to the labor force. However, millions of adult women, young people, and older people who have retired or can retire from work either do not work or seek work for part of the year. . . .

Although there are indications that willingness to move has diminished in recent years with the accumulation of . . . financial assets attached to the community, such as more general homeownership and increased rights to pensions and other benefits associated with seniority . . . in a particular firm, there is still a great deal of shifting both geographically and, to a more limited extent, occupationally. Young people, in particular, are willing to make changes; and the more education they have, the more readily they move.

Analysis of the occupations of the people now engaged directly in the defense effort in the United States . . . indicates a relatively high proportion in the professions and in the skilled occupations. As a group, they are relatively well educated. Moreover, they are generally younger . . . but still with some experience to count in their favor in finding a job. These characteristics of younger age, higher education, skill, and training are assets in readjustment. They should offset to some extent the problems attendant on the high degree of specialization in much of today's defense effort. . . .

Of the estimated 2.6 million persons employed directly and indirectly in all private industries providing defense goods and services in 1960, it is estimated that over 380,000 were professional and technical workers. Another 545,000 were skilled craftsmen. These proportions are very high relative to the national average, and employment prospects in these occupational fields are expected to expand rapidly over the next decade. On the other hand, over 30 per cent were semiskilled workers ("operatives"), as compared to under 20 per cent for all nonagricultural employment. For this group unemployment rates have been higher than average. Clerical workers, for whom demand is quite good, are in about the same proportion in defense as in all industries, while service workers and laborers— with an even higher rate of unemployment—are relatively less numerous.

OPPORTUNITIES FOR TRAINING AND RETRAINING

Opportunities for training and retraining arise in a variety of ways and from a variety of sources, including industry, local institutions, and state and federal programs. In large part the initiative rests with private individuals and business firms. Individuals voluntarily learn new skills and increase their knowledge by a variety of means—attending school formally or going to special classes in off hours or in the evening, taking correspondence courses, learning on the job. Private industry has extensive on-the-job training and retraining programs. . . . Some form of induction training is almost universal in large private enterprises, and many have extensive training programs for experienced workers. Thus, a large proportion of the persons now engaged in defense-related activities could expect to be trained or retrained by their new employers.

It has long been a policy of the government of the United States to encourage and help support certain types of vocational education and occupational training. Important among these is the vocational education system in the public high schools largely financed by local and state educational authorities with assistance from the federal government. Once directed primarily to young people already in school, attention has turned more recently to vocational training and retraining of out-of-school youth and adults. Increasingly this type of class has been used for training the unemployed. . . .

In addition, several states have established their own special programs for retraining the adult unemployed. . . .

The passage of the Area Redevelopment Act in 1961 established additional federal aid for the training of unemployed workers in areas with longstanding unemployment. . . . A much broader program, embodied in the Manpower Development and Training Act of 1962, was adopted in March 1962. It provides a nationwide opportunity for occupational training, with priority given to experienced unemployed persons who are heads of families. Training will also be given to employed persons to improve their skills. . . .

. . . The . . . Trade Expansion Act of 1962 . . . [is] of further relevance in this context. In addition to . . . assistance to industries adversely affected by imports, it also foresees the institution— where appropriate—of worker-training programs after vocational counseling and testing. . . .

. . . [Because] these measures are directed toward the relief of localized problems of unemployment, they should greatly strengthen the capabilities of the United States to help members of the civilian work force presently engaged in defense-related work to equip themselves for new jobs in the event of disarmament.

At the close of World War II and again at the close of the Korean War the government undertook massive programs for the education, training, and job placement of men and women discharged from the Armed Services. These programs, for which approximately $20 billion was spent, were exceedingly effective not only in restoring millions of individuals fairly promptly to a useful role in the economy of the country but also in providing extensive educational and technical training. . . .

Both . . . were on a very large scale, dealing with millions

of men—far more than are at present in the Armed Services. Both
were effective. Both have been appraised, and recommendations
for their improvement have been made. Experience in their administration provides a basis for planning similar programs to meet
future needs.

OTHER MEANS OF EASING THE ADJUSTMENT PROCESS
IN THE LABOR FORCE

Programs of training and retraining would need to be comple-
mented by a nationwide system for collecting information on employment opportunities and available manpower to facilitate the
matching of men with jobs. Extended unemployment compensation
for workers released by defense industries and for veterans, and
relocation grants or loans to help workers move to areas where the
employment opportunities are greatest are other possibilities. Here,
again, the . . . Trade Expansion Act of 1962, with its provision for
financing reasonable costs of relocating families in cases where the
head of the household is made unemployed by imports and has a
definite job offer elsewhere, could provide valuable practical experience in dealing with disarmament adjustment problems.

THE SPECIAL CASE OF RESEARCH AND DEVELOPMENT

. . . The release of scientists and engineers by defense industries should facilitate an acceleration of civilian research and development. Such an increase in research and development manpower
could be used with great benefit to society and yield high returns
in many industries where presently very little research and development is directed toward improving products or processes. The
civilian economy would benefit especially from increased long-
range research and experimentation with advanced technological
possibilities of the sort that the research teams presently employed
by defense industries have conducted so successfully.

It is, however, impossible to predict by how much private research support would increase in the event of disarmament. Certainly the increase would be substantial. It is likely, however, that,
in order to absorb the released research and development resources

smoothly and to help guide them to the highest priority uses, a positive government program would be required. . . .

. . . Some of the research and development resources freed by disarmament would no doubt be transferred to more substantial civilian atomic-energy and space programs. But there are also urgent needs or desirable goals for research and development in such fields as urban transportation, housing, health, education, and exploration and exploitation of the ocean resources.

Released research and development resources could also be used to great advantage to complement an expanded foreign-aid program. . . .

The freeing of research and development resources could be one of the most important economic benefits of disarmament. But here, as in other aspects, advance planning and coordinated action will minimize the transitional problems and make it possible to profit more extensively from the large opportunities which disarmament affords.

DISARMAMENT AND DOMESTIC NEEDS

The United States enjoys at this time a high level of economic well-being which is unprecedented and unparalleled. . . .

Yet, our very accomplishments . . . call to our attention the economic, social, and cultural needs which remain unmet. . . .

A significant part of the economic and social "shortfall" in the United States . . . [arises from] the substantial requirements for national defense. As these demands are progressively eliminated by an adequate and effective disarmament agreement, we can look for more rapid progress toward the economic and social goals which Americans set for themselves individually and collectively. . . . Even without disarmament we will cope more adequately with many of these civilian needs, but it is clear that progress could be much faster if the resources now devoted to defense could be freed for such uses. . . .

It is impossible to predict with any certainty how the American people will in fact employ the resources which would be released by . . . disarmament. In a free society such as ours, the individual values and preferences of each member will have a vital impact both on his own decisions . . . and on the decisions of his representatives in government. . . . The following discussion of some of the areas of civilian needs which are apparent today is intended to be illustrative of the opportunities which disarmament would present or enhance. It cannot be exhaustive, nor can it in any way prejudge the choices . . . which will eventually be made. . . .

Both individual and collective needs can be met by private or by governmental activity. In the United States the pattern which has been evolving through history includes a very large reliance on private initiative and a growing role for public programs; in some matters there is a close combination of the two. The discussion that follows is concerned primarily with suggesting the dimensions of certain needs which are of broad significance; the methods of satisfying them, whether by private effort, governmental programs—or a combination of the two—are incidental to this purpose.

Growth in Population and National Product

The [U.S.] Bureau of the Census projects an increase in the population of the United States from 180.6 million in 1960 to 244 million by 1980 and to 329 million by the year 2000. . . . Thus, during the 1960s the American labor force is expected to increase at roughly half again its rate of growth during the 1950s. . . . The economy will require progressively higher levels of education and skills in the working population. . . . It is also clear that new capital equipment will be required to complement the expanding labor force. Just to keep pace with the rate of increase in manpower will require capital investment of at least 7 per cent of GNP; if capital stock per employed person is to grow at a pace sufficient to permit productivity increases at the rate achieved during the 1950s, investment will have to be significantly higher than the 8.6 per cent of GNP used in this way in recent years. . . .

Residential Construction

. . . It is estimated that, if our growing population is to be supplied with enough housing to accommodate every American household in an adequate housing unit by the end of this decade, construction . . . expenditure would have to rise progressively to a level of

. . . $25 billion (1961 dollars) in 1970—an increase of roughly 50 per cent over 1961 levels. If construction of nonhousekeeping residential units were included, total expenditures . . . would come to $33 billion.

The . . . projection takes into account continuation of the population shift from rural to urban areas and replacement of demolitions . . . [arising from] public improvements and other causes. It assumes no change in the current vacancy rates, a slight improvement in the homeownership rate, and total elimination of dilapidated housing units.

Projections . . . suggest . . . we will attain the indicated housing goal in 1970 only if there is a significant addition to the resources which can now be reasonably expected to be allocated to housing construction over the decade. In particular this applies to housing for low-income groups requiring subsidization. Any savings from disarmament could therefore play an important role in this field.

Urban Needs

Population projections indicate that the urban population will increase in the current decade by about 36 million, compared with 29 million in the last decade. Within the metropolitan areas, the central cities are expected to show only a 15 per cent increase, . . . while the other urban places are expected to have a 63 per cent increase.

The implication . . . is a tremendous physical expansion of suburban areas which will require . . . capital improvements and increased . . . transportation facilities. The population growth of central cities will be concentrated substantially in those of rapidly expanding young metropolitan areas, while many of the older cities will continue to lose population as they did in the 1950-60 decade. For the revitalization of these older cities, a much higher level of urban-renewal assistance than is contemplated by present budgetary levels could be utilized. . . .

The ultimate potential of urban renewal in the United States is, indeed, very great. Many widely varying estimates have been made of cumulative totals that may some day be involved, differing according to assumptions of policy and cutoff dates. The primary

limitation is the prospective supply of capital for domestic investment that will be available within the structure of . . . [the GNP]
as it expands in the years ahead.

Total investment needs for urban transit and suburban railroad
plant and equipment during the current decade have recently been
estimated at almost $10 billion. . . . Thus, if the financial resources
were available, about $1 billion per year should be invested over
the decade in urban transit facilities to meet urban transportation
needs. Available data indicate that substantially less than this is
actually being invested. . . .

. . . Between 1958 and 1980, $108 billion would be required to
meet urban water and sewer needs. This would mean average
annual . . . expenditures of about $5 billion per year. In the last
few years, total contract awards (in current dollars) for construction of municipal water facilities and of sewer and sewage-treat-
ment facilities have ranged between $1 billion and $1.5 billion per
year. In order to meet the needs . . . adequately, . . . annual
. . . expenditures would have to be increased by between $3 billion
and $4 billion.

The need for expansion of educational and medical facilities is
discussed below. There will also be many other community needs—
such as for police and fire stations, public office buildings, and
recreational facilities—that will have to be met on a greatly expanded scale.

The Natural Resources Field

Projections of natural resources activities based wholly on future
needs have been tentative and fragmentary. Therefore only some
qualitative statements of future needs in the resources field and
some tentative estimates of the opportunities and needs for public
and private capital investments . . . during the next ten to twenty
years are presented here.

WATER RESOURCES DEVELOPMENT

As pointed out in the 1961 report of the Senate Select Committee on National Water Resources,[1] positive action needs to be

taken to develop and use the abundant resources placed in our custody and to develop the practices and techniques which will permit ever-increasing needs to be filled within the finite limits of the resources we have.

The report notes that while total requirements for withdrawal of water from lakes and streams . . . in 1954 was 300 billion gallons daily, or about 27 per cent of the total streamflow, withdrawals in 1980 would be about 559 billion gallons daily and, in the year 2000, more than 888 billion gallons daily, or more than 80 per cent of total streamflow.

The report of the Select Committee presented possible federal programs of water development for navigation, flood control, power generation, irrigation, municipal and industrial works for water supply and waste disposal, recreation, wildlife and fisheries protection; and state and local government and private development for power generation, municipal, industrial and rural domestic water supply, waste collection and treatment, and miscellaneous purposes. These programs up to 1980, which include those relating to urban water and sewage-disposal needs discussed above, would require federal expenditures of almost $55 billion and nonfederal expenditures of $173 billion in order to meet the requirements resulting from existing deficiencies, anticipated obsolescence, and growth.

OTHER RENEWABLE RESOURCES

Tentative projections by the Resources Program Staff, [U.S.] Department of the Interior, of what appear to be economically justified programs, . . . including some private activity, . . . in forestry, soil and watershed conservation, rangeland conservation, and park and recreational development, . . . indicate the desirability of expenditures substantially greater than present outlays for these purposes.

. . . A projected program of improvement of federal and state forest lands . . . would call for expenditures of $3.6 billion during a period of ten years. . . . A similarly projected ten-year program for soil and watershed conservation . . . would total $4.6 billion, probably including some overlapping of the projection of the Senate

Select Committee. . . . Conservation of federal range lands . . . would aggregate $1.2 billion. . . . A projected program. . . for management and protection, construction of improvements, and rehabilitation of existing facilities in the National Park System is estimated to cost $1.1 billion. It includes the "Mission 66" program of the National Park Service, which is designed to overcome by 1966 the lag in development of National Park System facilities which resulted from the practical cessation of construction during World War II and the slowdown in construction during the Korean conflict.

For additions to the National Park System, including seashore and lakeshore areas, scenic parks in Utah and Nevada, and a prairie national park in Kansas, the President in his recent conservation message recommended an eight-year program of land acquisition totaling $500 million. . . .

. . . An adequate program for improvement of habitat for migratory wildfowl and some upland game species and other construction and improvement in federal wildlife refuges, together with other measures for wildlife development, would cost $380 million, including $150 million for land acquisition, during a ten-year period.

TOTAL NATURAL RESOURCES PROGRAM

The total federal cost of these possible programs over a period of ten years would be at an annual rate of about $4 billion, or almost twice the current rate of expenditures for conservation and development of natural resources. In addition, the state, local-government, and industrial programs for water development alone are estimated by the Senate Select Committee on National Water Resources to cost about $8 billion annually. . . .

Educational Needs, 1970

In identifying educational needs, 1970 is only the day after tomorrow; all of the children who will then be enrolled in the fourth grade or higher have already been born, and those who will then be above the sixth grade are already in earlier stages of the educational process

MINIMUM NEEDS

A trend projection for 1970 indicates . . . the number of students in elementary and high school . . . will rise from 42.5 million in 1960 to 53 million in 1970 and the number . . . in institutions of higher learning will double to reach about 7 million. This assumes no change in the causal factors which determined attendance rates in the 1950s and no educational improvements as regards dropouts, staff-pupil ratio, or kindergarten enrollment.

Assuming present levels of the teaching art and technology and also present composition of educational costs, school enrollments in kindergarten through the twelfth grade by 1970 will require an annual expenditure of about 50 per cent more than the 1960-61 expenditures, which are estimated at about $20 billion. This estimate includes a major increase in investment for additional capital facilities, increased expenditures for the training and employment of additional teachers, and an increase in salaries of about 40 per cent over 1957-58 levels in order to compete for the required number of teachers. . . .

To accommodate the number of students . . . in institutions of higher learning, . . . with no change in present staff-student instructional and residential space ratios, would require total annual expenditures by 1970 of more than two and one half times present estimated expenditures of $6.7 billion. This, again, allows for major increases in annual outlay for capital facilities, and includes a salary increase of 50 per cent over 1957-58 levels, without which it would not be possible to compete for the necessary additional staff. . . .

IMPROVEMENT BEYOND TREND PROJECTIONS

The foregoing projections constitute pressing minimum educational needs for 1970 which will presumably be met whether there is disarmament . . . or not. However, the society and the economy of the 1970s will actually make greater demands on education.

The accelerating rate of technological innovation and additions to knowledge in various fields will call for more extended study by more people. Evolving social values and educational thinking will

place new emphasis on programs for students with both higher
and lower levels of talent, on the reduction of dropouts, . . . and
on provision for a significantly higher proportion of the more tal-
ented to obtain . . . higher education. . . . [T]he labor market
will increasingly favor those who offer better educational and training qualifications. Most important, however, would be the major
changes that would transpire if the deliberate decisions were made
. . . to invest heavily in education and to devise the *new kinds of
education* called for by the needs and the capacities of those portions of the population not now considered as part of the post-
secondary school clientele, and by the rising demands for highly
skilled and educated people that could be expected in the economy
and society of 1970. . . .

General application to elementary and secondary schools of such
qualitative improvements as the lowering of staff-pupil and class-
room-pupil ratios would, in conjunction with enrollment increases
indicated above, require massive investments, . . . perhaps almost
doubling capital outlays and increasing annual operating costs by
one third above those indicated for the . . . minimum needs.

There will also be a strong case for a sharp increase over trend
estimates for minimum needs in . . . post-high school education.
It is likely that the demand for education at the college and university levels will tend to increase at a rate greater than the rate
. . . in the 1950s. The need for postdoctoral study and mid-career
updating in the learned professional fields will also increase at
greater than trend rate.

. . . [O]lder forms of vocational education are likely to be absorbed in a variety of more educationally extensive, nondegree,
liberal and vocational, post-high school programs of from six
months' to three years' duration. . . . They would serve not only
the high school leavers but also those already in the work force
who are in need of additional skills and insights required for
transfer or upgrading in relation to individual development and
technological change. It is likely that within a few years the post-
high school category will constitute a major educational challenge. . . .

Health Services

. . . Progress toward a more completely available high level of medical care in the United States calls for a concerted attack on many fronts. It will depend on a larger supply of health personnel, a greater investment in health facilities, achievement of a greater degree of coordination among health services, and generation of more purchasing power through improved systems of financing personal health services. . . .

Basic to any expansion in health services is the availability of an adequate supply of well-trained health personnel. . . . In order even to maintain the existing ratios of physicians and dentists to the population, it is estimated that by 1970 it will be necessary not only to strengthen and expand existing medical and dental schools, but to establish, equip, and staff twenty to twenty-four new medical schools and twenty new dental schools. The cost of building these teaching facilities is estimated at $1 billion at present prices.

At present, the United States has 7.7 acceptable hospital beds of all types per 1000 persons in the population. Merely to maintain the same ratio as population expands will require the provision of more than 23,000 additional hospital beds each year throughout the next decade.

Beyond this, there is a need to increase present ratios and to replace obsolete plant and equipment. Scientific and technological changes have created new services and new methods of therapy requiring costly changes in physical plant. . . .

Increasing urbanization and the growth of the suburbs will require new construction and metropolitan planning for hospital and medical facilities. In addition there is a need for many new types of community facilities. The development of nursing homes providing skilled nursing care outside of a hospital setting is a relatively recent phenomenon. An increase in these and other facilities for chronic care is needed today and will be increasingly important as the proportion of aged persons in the population rises. . . .

. . . [A]ir-pollution control will require an intensified program of biological and engineering research to identify and measure harmful contaminants and determine their effects. At present the total national expenditure for air-pollution control is about $300-

$400 million per year. It is estimated that by 1970 the total expenditures should more than double.

The needs and opportunities as regards adequate water supplies and pollution control have already been noted. With more people, more industry, more processing, and more waste, the problem of solid-waste disposal is becoming more critical. Current total national expenditures for urban solid waste collection and disposal are approximately $2 billion annually. This rate will have to be raised by about 50 per cent to correct present unsatisfactory practices and to meet increasing needs.

. . . [R]eports . . . suggest that on the basis of capacity, long-range trends in support of research and other relevant factors, a national health research program of $3 billion in 1970 is feasible. If research facilities and personnel now devoted to defense-related research activities were to become available as a result of disarmament, it would be possible to step up research in the field of health and medical care much more rapidly than would otherwise be possible.

Social Security and Social Welfare

The United States has today an extensive system of public income-maintenance programs. These are supplemented by a wide range of private employee-benefit plans and other organized income-maintenance measures. . . .

Aggregate benefit payments under these programs have been rising as a percent[age] of the total national output, largely as a result of the expanding coverage and gradual maturing of the Old-Age, Survivors', and Disability Insurance (OASDI) system. . . .

Important and extensive as are the social-insurance protections now available, both the coverage and the level of benefits in many of the programs are less adequate than would be desirable. The general magnitude of desirable improvement in the expenditures involved can be illustrated by reference to some of the major programs.

The national . . . [OASDI] program now covers about 90 per cent of the active labor force. The number of beneficiaries will continue to increase fairly rapidly over the next few decades as an increasing proportion of those reaching retirement age have insured status.

Since 1950 the Congress has increased benefits under this program almost every two years. The changes since 1940, when benefits first began, have been more than sufficient to match increases in the general price level. They have been less than a third as large as increases in general wage levels during the period. If defense needs should continue to require tax revenues of the order of magnitude now prevailing, one might anticipate a similar trend in the future. In the event of disarmament, however, the nation may well decide that the aged, the disabled, and widows and children should share more equally in the increasing output of the economy. It has been estimated that, if the law were amended to increase benefit outlays in relation to increases in productivity, aggregate benefit payments in 1970 (in constant dollars) would be more than double the 1960 figure of $11.2 billion; without such a change it would be 60 per cent greater.

In 1960 private pension plans paid about $1.7 billion in pensions for retired workers. These payments also will increase in the future as more of the workers covered by relatively new plans retire. Very few private plans at present attempt to adjust benefits to changing price or wage levels. Furthermore, many of the workers now under private pension plans will not actually stay with the same employer long enough to acquire pension rights. Additional resources might well be directed toward the improvement of private pension benefits. . . .

PUBLIC ASSISTANCE

In any society, no matter how extensive its social-insurance program or other social measures, there will be some persons who are currently unable to meet from their own income and resources all of their basic living requirements. In the United States there are several public-assistance programs designed to provide a minimum income to needy individuals and families.

An expanding economy will reduce to some extent the need for public assistance, but there will presumably always remain older persons, marginal workers, broken families, and individuals with special needs who do not have the current income necessary for a socially acceptable level of living.

It is impossible to estimate with any degree of precision how many people in the United States are likely to need public assistance a decade from now. This will depend in considerable part on how need is then defined and on the extent to which the contribution of OASDI and other programs to meet the need may have been enlarged. Currently some 7 million persons are receiving public assistance. Assuming that, concurrent with the population increase, the standards of assistance will be raised as they have been in the past when general levels of living move upward, it could reasonably be expected that 7 million persons might also receive assistance in 1970.

A 1958 study, *Unmet Needs in Public Assistance*,[2] which measured assistance payments against a standard which provided only twice the amount needed for a low-cost food budget, a not very high standard, found that assistance expenditures for old-age recipients then on the rolls would have to increase by 6 per cent and for dependent children by 72 per cent. Extending such estimates to other categories of assistance, this analysis implies that an additional $1 billion could be spent today for public assistance, excluding the costs of medical care, to assure reasonable levels of living for dependent groups throughout the nation.

No ready basis exists for estimating the total amounts of medical care required by assistance recipients. Such care, however, is an important item of need among recipients of public aid, whose poverty results in health neglect that both causes and aggravates illness and disabilities. An estimate is available of the increase in expenditures . . . under old-age assistance and aid to dependent children that would have occurred in 1958 if all states had provided care similar . . . to the care provided . . . in the twenty-four states with costs above the national median. The annual increase would have amounted to $322 million, or almost 120 per cent. . . . [If we take] into account the other assistance programs, including the program of medical assistance for the aged, total medical-care expenditures through public assistance may need to undergo further substantial expansion. What amounts of medical care should be provided through public assistance will depend on the extent to which other public programs are available.

SOCIAL SERVICES

Community services in the United States have developed in a number of ways and been organized through both public and private agencies. . . . It is not possible to estimate either the total current expenditures on community and social services or the additional amounts that might be so used, but that a substantial expansion of many of these services is needed to meet the needs of a complex and growing urban economy is clear. Such expansion would require both increased expenditures of money and large increases in trained manpower.

. . . At present, about half of the counties in the United States lack the services of a public child-welfare worker. . . . Caseloads in many public-assistance agencies today are too large to allow time and attention for services that might help families to become self-supporting or better able to handle their own affairs. . . . Adequate day-care services for children would require public expenditures of possibly $60 million or about twelve times the amounts spent for this purpose at present. If homemaker services were available throughout the nation in the same ratio to population as now prevails in certain European countries, expenditures for such services would be at least $40 million, almost ten times what they are today.

The number of persons needing rehabilitation services to enable them to lead active productive lives is growing as the population increases and as an increasing number of our people live longer. The number of persons disabled annually who need vocational rehabilitation services in order to work is estimated at 275,000, and this number can be expected to increase. We are rehabilitating vocationally today about 100,000 disabled people. With greater resources, we could meet substantially more of the present and future needs for rehabilitation. Among other things, the training of professional personnel and research could be stepped up.

We shall undoubtedly spend increasing amounts for social services in any event, but the needed expansion will be greatly expedited if additional resources become available as a result of disarmament.

SOCIAL RESEARCH

In order to solve or mitigate the problems resulting from rapid social and economic change and to direct social policy more effectively toward our general welfare objectives, we need to step up both the scope and intensity of social research. A relatively small proportion of the total research expenditures of the federal government or of the academic institutions of the country goes for social research as compared with research in the natural sciences and in medicine. The amounts available for support of the social sciences and for research and demonstration projects in the social field have, however, increased in recent years.

There is a serious lack of trained research workers in the social sciences and in social research generally. The increasing availability of funds for social research should help somewhat to encourage more competent people to enter these fields. The trend toward greater encouragement and support of social research could be speeded up by the proper direction of the research funds, facilities, and potential that would be released by disarmament.

Most of the above examples of domestic civilian needs to which the savings achieved under disarmament might be applied would call for increased allocation of public funds. Many of them would, however, also require substantial private expenditure. Quite generally it is, in fact, to be anticipated that increased private consumption and investment would employ a substantial portion of the resources which will be released by disarmament.

It should also be observed that, . . . [although] disarmament could contribute significantly to progress in the satisfaction of the civilian needs outlined in this chapter, the effect on aggregate demand and on employment, of new or larger expenditures to meet these needs, will differ from case to case. These differences in economic effect will, of course, have a bearing on the choice of measures which must be adopted to offset the decline in defense demand. . . .

NOTES

1. S. Rept. 29, 87th Cong., 1st sess., published January 31, 1961.

2. *Social Security Bulletin* (April 1960), 3-11.

DEFENSE CUTS BRING A NEW KIND
OF JOB CRISIS

U.S. News & World Report

*This report on the immediate effects of defense cutbacks con-
trasts with the long-range view of the third article. The "new kind of
job crisis" refers to the unemployment of highly educated and skilled
scientists and engineers caused by the partial reductions in defense expenditures occurring in 1964. Of course, later events may
well make the situations described only temporary and the forecasts
incorrect. Reprinted from "U.S. News & World Report," published
at Washington (May 18, 1964 issue).*

Cutbacks in defense spending are creating a new—and growing
—class of unemployed in this country.

The new jobless group: engineers, scientists, technicians, and
highly skilled craftsmen.

Layoffs have already reached into the tens of thousands. More
layoffs are in prospect as arms spending heads lower in the months
ahead.

Highly trained specialists, many with advanced college degrees,
are pounding the streets—shoulder to shoulder with the school
dropout and the laborer.

Defense firms, too, are feeling the pinch of arms cutbacks. So are
entire communities in key defense areas around the nation.

To get a measure of the growing impact of defense-spending
reductions, *U.S. News & World Report* sent staff members out
around the country to talk with unemployed workers, union officials, company presidents, personnel specialists and experts in the
problems of the defense industry.

FACTOR: "GRADUAL PEACE"

From all sides come reports of a looming surplus of engineers and scientists as defense industries are forced to adjust to "gradual peace."

Says Terence McCarthy, Vice President of Basic Economic Appraisals, Inc., in New York City:

We are going to get massive unemployment in pockets—those areas where defense production is dominant. That would be around shipyards, defense-production centers on the East, West and Gulf Coasts.

Arms cuts today will be much more difficult on people and companies than after World War II. Then, people had plenty of cash and debt was small. Today, nobody's got any cash and everybody's got a mortgage.

The same prediction of high unemployment in the wake of big defense cuts is made by Murray L. Weidenbaum, senior economist for Stanford Research Institute. He sees "pockets of unemployment" in defense areas similar to those of the Appalachian coal-mining or the New England textile regions.

Manpower experts estimate that about three out of every five scientists and engineers in the country are engaged in activities related to national defense.

Now defense is pulling back as a customer and as a source of jobs. . . .

Nearly all major spending programs will feel the bite—from missiles and aircraft to ships and research projects.

ONLY THE BEGINNING

It's all part of an economy drive ordered by Defense Secretary Robert McNamara. And the cuts are just beginning. Shape of things to come was outlined in a May 6th speech by Secretary McNamara when he forecast a $4 billion cut in defense spending by 1967.

As the flow of dollars out of the Pentagon slows, many companies are slashing payrolls.

Says Christos T. Christy, President of the Engineers and Scientists Guild at Lockheed in Burbank, Calif[ornia]: "An engineer today has no more security than the migrant farm workers of the 1930s."

From Carl A. Frische, President of Sperry Gyroscope on New York's Long Island: "The entire defense industry is heading for a shake-out—overcapacity is growing, profits are shrinking—and the inevitable byproduct of a shake-out is fewer jobs."

Sperry Gyroscope has laid off 300 engineers and scientists during the past fifteen months—along with 1100 production and clerical workers.

In New Jersey, more than 20,000 engineers, technicians, and production workers in defense industries have lost their jobs in the last fourteen months.

The Arma Division of American Bosch Arma Corporation, on Long Island, had the job of developing the guidance system for the Atlas missile. Now that contract is phasing out—with no new ones to take its place—so Arma is making big cuts in jobs.

Sample: More than 1100 engineers and technicians have received "pink slips" in the past fifteen months.

"ENGINEERS SELLING BOATS"

Says Sanford Lenz, Vice President of the engineers' union at Arma: "In the depression we had Ph.D.'s selling apples. It's almost as bad today. We've got engineers with degrees selling boats on weekends to earn a buck."

Boeing Company, in Seattle, had nearly 76,000 workers in aerospace work in August 1962. At latest count, employment had fallen below 55,000—and it's still dropping.

One reason: cancellation by the Defense Department of the "Dyna-Soar" space-glider contract. From that one cancellation alone, about 1000 engineers and scientists will be let go by Boeing.

Note this: Boeing officials say that, for the first time since World War II, the company now is making major reductions in scientists and engineers.

In Sunnyvale, Calif[ornia], forty miles south of San Francisco, where the Polaris missile is built by Lockheed, the firm's employment has dropped by nearly 2000 since January, and layoffs are continuing at the rate of one hundred a week.

From a spokesman for a defense contractor in the Boston area:

"Nearly all the companies here along Route 128 are hit bad. We're a small outfit, so we are especially vulnerable. We've got one contract left. If that goes, we go out of business."

Boston's Raytheon Company, deep in defense electronics, has laid off 4600 defense workers in the past year. Included in the layoffs are many highly skilled technical workers.

SKILLED "GETTING THE AX"

This picture of the job market for engineers and scientists today is provided by David O'Brian, personnel specialist, of Medford Lakes, N[ew] J[ersey]:

People with top skills are getting the ax. I cover the market from Boston to Baltimore and I see it everywhere.

When the going was easy, when defense contracts were on the rise, companies were desperate. A big contractor would send a plane to an employment agency, fill it up with engineers and fly them back to the plant. Pay was high. Raises came big, and often.

Now that's all changed. Contracts are fading. Companies are dumping workers—especially those who are overpaid for their real ability. The engineer making $16,000 but worth only $11,000 is not getting a pay cut—he's being dropped.

Really able people are being lopped off, too. I know of some layoffs that have reached into the upper echelon of smaller companies.

MISLEADING ADS

Mr. O'Brian says that columns of help-wanted ads for engineers and scientists often are misleading. His comment:

Don't let those ads fool you. Many of them are just there to keep the name of the company before the labor market in case a contract should come through. Other firms are just collecting résumés for the future, not actually hiring unless they find a guy with exactly the qualifications they want.

The market for engineers is really soft. The electronics industry, long a defense baby, is getting back to normal.

How badly are communities being hit by the arms cutbacks?

Listen to Rocco Campanaro, Executive Vice President of the Long Island Federation of Labor:

Long Island is in danger of becoming a depressed area. Our economy on the Island is built on defense. Now, with contract cancellations, practically every defense plant is being clobbered.

Wives are having to take jobs to keep the family going. Workers with twenty years' seniority are getting the gate. We're not Appalachia, but the situation is critical.

"PEOPLE TAKING LICKING"

Says Mr. O'Brian, the personnel specialist: "In my town of Medford Lakes, not far from Camden, there are 300 homes for sale out of a total of 1200. People can't sell without taking a big licking. It's rough."

In the Seattle area most large building developments are feeling the impact of the Boeing layoffs. Building permits for single-family dwellings in Seattle and unincorporated areas of King County during January and February amounted to $8.7 million, only about half as high as a year earlier.

Sales of used homes are slow, particularly in the $15,000-$25,000 class. Some older homes stand empty. Mortgage foreclosures are up. Merchants report store sales are lagging behind a year ago.

From the head of a machine shop in a Seattle suburb: "The outlook is grim."

In February, Lockheed closed its Van Nuys, Calif[ornia] plant, laid off 1400 workers and transferred 700 people to its Sunnyvale plant. All types of business in the area now are feeling the loss of Lockheed's $13 million payroll.

A spokesman for Radio Corporation of America, in Camden, N[ew] J[ersey], notes that defense cutbacks have forced layoffs of 7500 company employes in the past two years. He adds: "Camden is hurting. The housing market is quite soft. Pentagon cutbacks reach out, indirectly, to every storekeeper in town."

Talk with unemployed engineers and scientists, and you get an idea of the personal impact of a defense cutback.

OUT AFTER TWENTY-TWO YEARS

This comment was made by an engineer who had been in defense work twenty-two years: "I've been out of a job since last July. I was making $13,000 a year, but I've offered to work for half that. No luck. One personnel chief refused to take me on for a $7000 job on the ground that I would be bored. He said I would know more than the boss in my section, that I'd be unhappy and soon quit. I wish he'd let me be the judge of that."

Or take the case of a senior engineer laid off from a Long Island defense firm: He made the rounds of other firms to no avail. Finally he was offered a job as "mechanical supervisor" at an exhibit at the nearby New York World's Fair.

"I'm just a glorified mechanic," he says, "but it's a job."

General Electric Company in 1963 had defense sales of $1 billion —equal to about 22 per cent of its total sales.

GE has already felt the impact of defense reductions, and more cuts are coming. Latest example: GE's Hanford atomic-products operation in Richland, Wash[ington]. Reduced output of plutonium at Hanford, ordered by the Atomic Energy Commission, will mean 2000 layoffs for GE workers beginning in January—mostly scientific and technical people.

What does GE do for those laid off? Says Olav Sorenson, personnel specialist for GE:

We try very hard to place these workers elsewhere in the company, and we have had pretty good luck.

We send the laid-off employe a letter—we call it a hunting license— which tells him how to go about applying for a job in some other part of the company. Or, if he desires, with some other firm.

It takes, usually, about three months to get relocated in a new job elsewhere in GE. Sometimes these people get outside offers sooner, so they leave us. It's a free country.

Part of the growing unemployment problem among highly skilled workers, companies report, can be attributed to the unwillingness of workers to move to new jobs.

Says one company president in Boston: "We know physicists, chemists, electrical engineers walking the streets for work because they are determined not to leave the Boston area."

From an employe at the Hanford plutonium works, when told of the coming cutback in jobs: "We were terrified. The best years of our lives and our fortunes are tied to this area. We don't want to leave."

In some cases defense workers are finding that they are too specialized to fit readily into civilian industry.

Says an RCA official: "Many of our top scientific people in defense work just can't handle jobs in our color-TV production lines in the Midwest. Besides, we don't have a big surplus of jobs going begging out there."

From Seymour Melman, Professor of Industrial Engineering at Columbia University: "The criteria of civilian work are so dramatically different from those of military work that initial retraining will be required for all levels of management, technicians, and workers. The men in military work have generated a trained incapacity for minimizing cost, either in design or in production."

A management-consultant firm recently compared research costs under defense contracts with those for commercial markets.

What the firm found was this: the typical defense-research operation requires four to five times as many scientists per sales dollar as the normal commercial operation.

Few companies, so far, have had much success in reducing their heavy dependence on defense business by getting into civilian lines.

Says Carl Frische, President of Sperry Gyroscope: "It would be difficult to find or name any significant example of the defense-oriented segment or company which has successfully converted from military production to industrial or consumer activity."

FROM CANOES TO COFFINS

Officials of the aerospace industry estimate that companies have lost three quarters of a billion dollars since 1960 trying to convert to some sort of peacetime industry. These ventures have ranged from producing everything from computers and canoes to coffins.

Where companies are having some success in acquiring more civilian business, progress is slow.

Example: Bendix Corporation. The company's sales ratio is 68 per cent military to 32 per cent civilian—compared with 70:30 a year ago. Says one spokesman for Bendix: "Good acquisitions in civilian lines are hard to come by."

Could the space program be stepped up to provide jobs for technical people no longer needed in arm industries?

The answer you get: Not very likely. Space spending, only one tenth the size of arms spending anyway, is seen leveling off, not rising. "Congress, and the people, wouldn't buy a big step-up in spending just to explore the outer galaxies," says one lawmaker.

How about massive public works? Again, strong doubts are expressed—at least in terms of providing many jobs for scientists and engineers.

Says Murray Weidenbaum, of Stanford Research: "A massive $5 billion or $15 billion program of new public works is not likely to effectively utilize the nuclear physicists, aerodynamicists, propulsion engineers, or other specialized personnel engaged in defense research, development, and production."

Meanwhile, layoffs are mounting as the economy mood grips the Pentagon.

And it's a new, elite group that is joining the ranks of the unemployed.

PART III

Can We Beat Our Swords into Plowshares?

THE TRANSFERABILITY OF DEFENSE INDUSTRY RESOURCES TO CIVILIAN USE

Murray L. Weidenbaum

Murray Weidenbaum has contributed much to the literature on the economic impact of defense expenditures, including their impact on the nation, on industries, and on regions. For several years he was a corporate economist with the Boeing Company, one of the nation's leading defense contractors; later he joined the staff of Stanford Research Institute. He has also been a member of the Panel on Economic Impacts of Disarmament for the U.S. Arms Control and Disarmament Agency, and Executive Secretary of the President's Committee on the Economic Impact of Defense and Disarmament. He is currently on the faculty of Washington University in St. Louis. The following statement was originally presented to the U.S. Senate Committee on Labor and Public Welfare in November 1963. It is reprinted here by permission of Murray L. Weidenbaum. (Printed in Nation's Manpower Revolution, *Hearings, Part 9 [Washington, D.C.: USGPO, 1964], pp. 3143-49.)*

INTRODUCTION

But while strongly insisting on the great advantages of peace, and the reduction of military and naval expenditure, it is quite as essential to assure that so long as present conditions last, a well organized and effective system of defense is a necessary part of State expenditure . . . to maintain a due balance between the excessive demands of alarmists and military officials, and the undue reductions in outlay sought by the advocates of economy, is one of the difficult tasks of the statesman.

C. F. Bastable, *Public Finance* (1895)

This paper is based on the assumption—which may be hypothetical—that a major shift will occur in the size and/or composition of the defense budget. I am not recommending any specific budget levels, other than those necessary to maintain the national security.

If a major reduction in defense spending is consistent with the national security, it would represent both a tremendous opportunity and also a yet unsolved problem of major proportions.

It is quite simple to take, for example, a hypothetical reduction in defense spending of, say, $10 billion and point out that these funds could be used to double the annual expenditure level in the United States on men's and boys' clothing, or to give each household a brand-new refrigerator, or to permit a reduction in federal income taxes of $200 for each taxpayer.

However, human wants are insatiable. A "wish list" of alternatives to defense expenditures might readily encompass most categories of public as well as private demand. The real problem is on the supply side—the limitations to resource mobility and the barriers that business firms face in entering or even in trying to leave individual sectors or industries of the economy.

This statement presents some information concerning the supply side—dealing with the lack of mobility in the sector of our nation's economy devoted to producing goods and services for the defense program.

I will then examine what I interpret to be some of the hard questions involved in determining the alternatives to defense expenditures; namely: What are the practical alternate uses for the resources currently devoted to the defense program? What basic modifications of public policy are required?

THE SPECIALIZED NATURE OF DEFENSE RESOURCES

As a first step in analyzing the specialized nature of defense resources, it is helpful to examine the degree of concentration of defense work in the private economy. Seventy-two per cent of the value of the military prime contracts awarded in the fiscal year

1962 went to one hundred companies and institutions. Within this amount, seven major industry groups account for over nine tenths of the value of the contracts awarded—aircraft, electrical and electronic equipment, oil refining, automobiles, construction, rubber, and ship-building, in that order.

Fifty-six of the one hundred companies are engaged directly in aircraft, missile, and space work, or in electronics and research and development work closely related to aircraft and missile programs. Ten of the hundred are suppliers of aviation gasoline and other petroleum products. Seven each are automotive, ship-building, ammunition, and service companies; five are construction firms, and one is a rifle producer.

Of greater significance is the relative importance of defense work to each of these industries and to the companies in these industries. For example, although the oil companies rank high as defense suppliers, military sales only account for about 10 per cent of the industry's output and a reduction in defense sales would involve only marginal adjustment problems. In contrast, for four industries, defense work represents from one half to all of the output. The conversion problems here would clearly be of a totally different order of magnitude. It is likely that the heart of the adjustment problem would center on these industries: ordnance (including missiles), aircraft, ship-building, and electronics.

Table 1 is an attempt to show the dependence of individual companies in these and related industries on defense-space orders. Because the proportion of company sales to the government is not reported by many defense contractors, an approximation method has been used. Essentially, the table shows the amount of prime contracts received from the [U.S.] Department of Defense and the National Aeronautics and Space Administration [NASA] by the thirty-five companies with the largest volume of such contracts. The combined defense-space orders of each of these companies is then expressed as a percentage of their sales for their last fiscal year, to provide a rough approximation of the importance of this business to these firms.

The limitations of this approach need to be kept in mind, particularly the fact that the production orders received in a given year normally result in sales in subsequent years. Nevertheless, the data in Table 1 show that some major defense contractors derive the

Table 1

Importance of Defense-Space Orders to Thirty-five Major Contractors:
Fiscal Year 1962
(in millions of dollars)

Company	(1) Defense Contracts	(2) NASA Contracts	(3) Total (1) + (2)	(4) Company Sales*	(5) Ratio of Orders to Total Sales (3)/(4) (per cent)
75-100 per cent:					
Republic Aviation Corp.	$ 332.8	$ 6.9	$ 339.7	$ 295.8	100.0+
McDonnell Aircraft Corp.	310.9	68.5	379.4	390.7	97.11
Grumman Aircraft Engineering Corp.	303.6	24.6	328.2	357.1	91.91
Lockheed Aircraft Corp.	1419.5	5.0	1424.5	1753.1	81.27
AVCO Corp.	323.3	1.4	324.7	414.3	78.37
North American Aviation, Inc.	1032.5	199.1	1231.6	1633.7	75.39
Hughes Aircraft Corp.	234.2	9.2	243.4	**	†
50-74 per cent:					
Collins Radio Co.	150.1	3.7	153.8	207.8	74.01
Thiokol Chemical Corp.	178.3	0.8	179.1	255.8	70.02
Raytheon Co.	406.6		406.6	580.7	70.02
Newport News Shipbuilding & Dry Dock Co.	185.0		185.0	267.3	69.21
Martin Marietta Corp.	802.7	1.8	804.5	1195.3	67.31
Boeing Co.	1132.8	15.6	1148.4	1768.5	64.94
General Dynamics Corp.	1196.6	27.9	1224.5	1898.4	64.50
Curtiss-Wright Corp.	144.6		144.6	228.7	63.23
United Aircraft Corp.	662.7	34.1	696.8	1162.1	59.96
Douglas Aircraft Co., Inc.	365.6	68.4	434.0	749.9	57.87
25-49 per cent:					
American Machine & Foundry Co.	187.3		187.3	415.4	45.09
General Tire & Rubber Co.	366.1	66.4	432.5	959.8	45.06
Northrop Corp.	152.5	1.3	153.8	347.5	44.26
Hercules Powder Co.	181.6		181.6	454.8	39.93
Sperry Rand Corp.	465.6	2.2	467.8	1182.6	39.56
Bendix Corp.	285.9	19.4	305.3	788.1	38.74
FMC Corp.	160.4		160.4	506.5	31.67
Pan American World Airways, Inc.	146.7		146.7	503.9	29.11
0-24 per cent:					
International Telephone & Telegraph Corp.	243.6	2.2	245.8	995.5	24.69
General Electric Co.	975.9	23.0	998.9	4792.7	20.84
Radio Corp. of America	339.6	20.2	359.8	1742.7	20.65
Westinghouse Electric Corp.	246.0	3.4	249.4	1954.5	12.76
International Business Machines Corp.	155.5	12.6	168.1	1925.2	8.73
American Telephone & Telegraph Corp.	467.7	10.8	478.5	11742.4	4.07
Ford Motor Co.	269.1		269.1	8089.6	3.33
General Motors Corp.	449.0	1.4	450.4	14640.2	3.08
Standard Oil Co. (New Jersey)	180.1		180.1	9537.3	1.89

* Net sales for fiscal year ending during 1962.

** Not available.

† Estimated from other sources to be in excess of 75 percent.

Note. In some cases, it appears that the ratio of defense-space orders to total sales in fiscal year 1962 is not an accurate indicator of the actual ratio of military-space sales to total sales.

bulk of their business from commercial sources, while others are primarily dependent on government work. Clearly, companies like A. T. & T., Ford, and General Motors devote a relatively small portion of their efforts to defense-space work, while North American Aviation, Republic, and McDonnell are heavily committed.

The adjustment problem would be compounded by the fact that the four cited industries cluster in a few regions of the country and represent a major part of the industrial base of these areas. In seven states the employment in the above four defense-related industries accounts for one fifth or more of total manufacturing employment, and for a much larger share of the postwar employment growth: Kansas, Washington, California, New Mexico, Connecticut, Arizona, and Utah, in that order.

The concentration is far greater in individual metropolitan areas such as Los Angeles, San Diego, Wichita, and Seattle.

Another aspect of the problem is the very specialized nature of the resources used by the major defense supplying companies. In contrast with the situation during World War II, and even with that during the Korean conflict, a far greater share of defense production today is performed in highly specialized facilities which have been specifically built for the purpose, often at the initiative of the military establishment, which still retains title to the factories and the equipment in it.

For example, four fifths or more of the equipment of the armies that took the field at the outbreak of World War I consisted of standard peacetime goods produced in ordinary peacetime production facilities. By 1941, almost one half of the total material needs of warfare consisted of special-purpose equipment. However, the bulk of this was still material that could be produced by converting ordinary peacetime facilities. Currently, about 90 per cent of the material needs of defense consists of specialized equipment which is produced in special facilities built for the purpose.

Moreover, the companies involved were set up for—and their experience is limited to—the design and production of military weapon systems and related aerospace vehicles. As a consequence of the technical requirements of military work, these companies have tremendous numbers of scientists and engineers compared to the commercial-oriented industries. The typical defense company hires four or five times the number of scientists and engineers than the most technically oriented commercial company to support the same volume of sales.

The National Science Foundation reports that aircraft and missile companies alone employ more scientists and engineers on research and development work than the combined total of the chemical, drug, petroleum, motor-vehicle, rubber, and machinery industries.

On the assumption that the work performed bears a definite relationship to the source of the funds, a rough approximation can be made as to the number of scientific personnel on defense-space work.

The National Science Foundation reports that 58 per cent of the research and development expenditures of private industry were financed by the federal government in 1962 and that 90 per cent of these are contributed by the [U.S.] Department of Defense and . . . [NASA]. Hence, approximately 52 per cent of total industry research and development (58 per cent times 90 per cent) is performed for defense-space purposes.

Applying this proportion to the 339,400 engineers and scientists doing research and development work in American industry, as of January 1963, yields the conclusion that 52 per cent—or 176,500—were engaged on projects funded by defense-space programs.

Let us examine the extent to which the specialized resources of the defense companies have been utilized in producing goods and services for the commercial economy.

THE LOCKED-IN NATURE OF DEFENSE RESOURCES

Since the end of World War II, many major defense contractors have sought to diversify their operations into commercial lines of business. The motives were numerous and varied over time—to compensate for a declining military market, to offset the fluctuations in military budgets, to enter more profitable areas, and to adjust for shifts within the military market.

These companies attempted to utilize the technological capabilities developed in the course of their military work to design and produce a great variety of commercial items. These included—

among many, many others—aluminum sport boats, prosthetic devices, stainless steel caskets, heavy-duty land vehicles, adhesives, wall panels, welding equipment, gas turbine engines, and cargo-handling systems. These efforts literally ranged from canoes to computers to coffins.

With one major exception, these diversification attempts have each been relatively small in comparison with [the production of] military equipment. The exception, of course, is transport aircraft for the commercial airlines. The large jetliners, the DC-8's, the 707's, and the 880's, have each involved large numbers of scientists, engineers, and other employees, and the resultant unit sales prices are comparable with [those of] many military products. However, the profit performance on these jet programs has been extremely poor. The losses incurred have both depleted the venture capital available to seek other commercial businesses and have reduced the enthusiasm of other defense companies to diversify.

Other than the few firms selling to the airlines, the large defense suppliers—especially in the aerospace field—have reported commercial sales of 1 or 2 per cent, or even less, over the years. The list of abandoned commercial ventures is a long and constantly growing one. The surviving efforts continue generally at marginal levels—either actually losing money, barely breaking even, or showing profit results considerably below military levels.

A variety of reasons is usually given for the inability of the large specialized defense companies to utilize their resources in commercial endeavors: their lack of marketing capability and their inability to produce large numbers of items of low unit price.

These weaknesses are not necessarily handicaps in defense and space work, where other capabilities are more important. For example, the lack of commercial marketing capability of these firms results from their preoccupation with meeting the rigorous technical requirements of the military customer. Their inability to produce large volumes at low cost also reflects their unique capability to design small numbers of large-scale systems of great technical complexity.

Even if we examine companies that have divisions producing weapon systems as well as commercial-product divisions, we find little transference of either personnel or product ideas from military to commercial work within the same company. A company's commercial departments may be hiring engineers, while simultaneously a military department may be laying off experienced technical personnel. Many knowledgeable persons contend that the environment of military weapon-system design and production is fundamentally different from—and, hence, the experience is rarely useful in—commercial enterprises. In the former, technical advance is often the prime and essential output, while in the latter, price is a critical parameter. A new model of refrigerator at half the price of current types may have a large market even if it suffers from significant reductions in quality. The second-best missile, in contrast, may hardly be a bargain. The comparison, of course, is oversimplified, but it illustrates the different nature of product innovation characteristic of commercial competition as compared to technological competition in the military field.

A large majority of the technical personnel who leave a company doing defense work go to other firms similarly engaged on defense contracts. There is some movement of professional and technical personnel from universities and other industries to defense work, but relatively little movement in the opposite direction. Differences in pay scale and degree of challenge in the work are often cited as barriers to movement from military to commercial or other work.

It may be helpful to note that, for a typical company producing aicraft and missiles, engineers and related technical personnel no longer constitute merely a single important but limited department, but may exceed in actual numbers the total of factory or "blue-collar" employment. In good measure, the major military contractors have become primarily large aggregations of research and development resources.

The alternate utilization ot these resources, in the event of a substantial reduction in defense requirements, would present an important issue of public policy.

CHANGES IN PUBLIC POLICY

There are two major categories of public policy which may be relied upon to help transfer defense-industry resources to nondefense pursuits. One category of federal programs and policies covers various attempts to aid defense contractors in diversifying into commercial markets. The other consists of efforts to transfer the research and development and other resources of defense contractors to companies and organizations in other parts of the economy. Both of these types of actions would, of course, be enhanced by effective application of general monetary and fiscal policies which would maintain the over-all levels of demand, income, and employment in the nation.

Given a cutback in defense spending, there is a variety of actions which, it has been suggested, the federal government could undertake to help defense contractors diversify. These include awarding them large amounts of nondefense research and development contracts or even establishing new requirements for nondefense goods which these companies could produce and sell to the government.

Also, under existing military contracts, the [U.S.] Department of Defense could do several things which would currently increase the commercial capability of defense contractors, such as treating commercial-product planning as an allowable cost on military contracts. This would provide a financial inducement to defense contractors to perform initial commercial studies while still engaged in defense work.

Defense-industry executives state that there are major civilian pursuits where their massive engineering competence is needed and could be employed. Examples cited include large-scale construction, mining of the ocean floor, sea-farming, further air and space travel, integration of transportation systems, revitalizing of the merchant marine, improved communications and weather forecasting, nuclear electric power, salt-water conversion, air-traffic-control systems, air- and water-pollution control, urban development, and programs of technical assistance to developing countries.

Government actions designed to aid the individual defense companies in converting to civilian activities may be the most direct and effective way of absorbing potential unemployment in the defense industries and of meeting the short-run requirements of economic stability. However, does sole reliance upon this course of action provide the best long-run reorientation and utilization of the resources currently employed in the defense sector? Is this approach to short-run economic adjustment consistent with maximum long-run economic growth and progress?

Faced with the difficulties encountered by the select business organizations which produce military weapon systems to penetrate commercial markets, it may be questionable public policy to invest very large amounts of government funds in motivating such endeavors. In view of the tremendous concentration of research and development in these companies, attention might well be given to the desirability and possibility of transferring some of these resources to other parts of the economy. Such action could have tremendous long-term benefits for the currently "underresearched" industries.

In contrast to the oft-voiced claims of private affluence amidst public poverty, research and development may be an important case of the reverse situation. The bulk of the research and development performed in the United States at the present time—65 per cent in 1962—is done pursuant to contracts with or grants from the federal government. Moreover, the portion represented by privately initiated and funded research and development has declined during the past decade—from 47 per cent in 1954 to 35 per cent in 1962.

Along these lines, it seems to be clear that the demonstration effect on private industry of the massive government expenditures on research and development may have already passed. The growth of company-funded research and development appears to have slowed down during the last few years, despite continued expansion in military and other federal research and development outlays. Compared to annual increases of 33 per cent in 1956 and 10-11 per cent during 1959 and 1960, company-funded research and development rose 3 per cent in 1961 and 6 per cent in 1962.

Hence, these seem to be relatively small pent-up private demands for the research and development resources currently devoted to the defense program. We cannot expect that a major reduction in military research and development expenditures will automatically lead to any significant increase in private outlays for research and development.

However, to the extent that the cost of research and development to an individual business firm can be reduced, private industry would increase its demand for research and development. Mechanisms for so reducing the cost of research and development include (1) a tax rebate similar to the tax credit recently enacted to encourage business firms to increase investment in producers durable equipment, (2) an aid program similar to the mining-exploration program of the [U.S.] Department of the Interior whereby the government pays part or all of the cost, but is reimbursed out of the proceeds of the results—if the research and development leads to profitable production, and (3) loan and loan guarantees similar to those of the Small Business Administration and the Export-Import Bank.

Several operational questions would arise, of course. What is the elasticity of private demand for research and development? Even if it is made a freed good, will the demand rise sufficiently to offset a major defense cutback?

Many of these and other alternatives would involve a number of government departments and agencies, and both the legislative and executive branches. These various alternative courses of action raise serious questions of national policy. Would the concern of the federal government with commercial-product development be an acceptable extension of the role of government in the American economy? Would some important characteristics of a private-enterprise economy be sacrificed?

If, as a nation, we are to come up with useful, acceptable, and timely answers to questions like these, public discussion and consideration need to begin. In the event of a significant decline in defense spending, it would appear that the resultant surplus of valuable resources, particularly research and development, would call for a broad long-range national program to encourage the development of alternate demands.

The major elements of such a program include:

1. Developing public policy on (a) the utilization of the resources that would become available and (b) the respective roles of private industry and federal, state, and local governments.

2. Assigning responsibilities to the various government agencies involved—Treasury, Commerce, Labor, the Council of Economic Advisers, the Office of Science and Technology, the Arms Control and Disarmament Agency, as well as the Department of Defense.

3. Developing mechanisms for carrying out these responsibilities, such as some of those suggested above, which would operate

in the private sector of the economy as well as in the public sector.

Summary

1. The conversion of defense-industry resources to peacetime pursuits would present both a tremendous opportunity as well as a problem of major proportions.

2. The heart of the adjustment problem would center on four industries, the bulk of whose sales go to the government: ordnance, aircraft, ship construction, and electronics.

3. The adjustment problem would be compounded because these four industries cluster in a few regions—notably the West Coast— where they represent a major part of the industrial base of these areas.

4. Moreover, the resources used by these industries for defense work are extremely specialized; relatively minor portions of either the people or the facilities have ever been "converted" to civilian work in the past.

5. With a few exceptions, the large specialized defense companies have not been successful in utilizing their technical capability to penetrate civilian markets.

6. Hence, government actions which have been suggested to assist defense contractors in commercial diversification to offset a defense cutback may be of limited effectiveness.

7. In view of the concentration of the nation's research and development in these companies, attention might be given to transferring some of these resources to other parts of the economy with possible long-term benefits for the "underresearched" industries.

8. The federal government could encourage all private industry to increase its demand for research and development through such mechanisms as a tax credit, joint financing, loans and loan guarantees, and technical assistance.

9. A long-range national program to encourage the development of alternate demands for any potentially surplus defense-industry resources would require: (a) developing public policy on utilizing the resources that would become available, and the respective roles of industry and government, (b) assigning responsibilities to the

various government agencies involved, defense as well as nondefense, and (c) developing mechanisms, such as those suggested, for carrying out these responsibilities both in the private sector as well as in the public sector.

THE DISARMAMENT OUTLOOK
FOR A LARGE DEFENSE CONTRACTOR

Lockheed Aircraft Corporation

Few large firms in the American economy are as defense-oriented as the Lockheed Aircraft Corporation. In fiscal years 1962 and 1963, it ranked first in the country in the value of prime contracts awarded. The following statement is a sample of the attitudes of such specialized firms toward disarmament and the transition problems it would bring them. The statement is especially interesting for the list of possible alternative uses for specialized defense resources. The reader should bear in mind that neither Lockheed's situation, including its diversification, nor its thinking is exactly representative of other large defense contractors. The statement was presented to the U.S. Senate Committee on Labor and Public Welfare in November 1963 (Printed in Nation's Manpower Revolution, Hearings, Part 9 [Washington, D.C.: USGPO, 1964], pp. 3049-54.) It is reprinted here by permission of Lockheed Aircraft Corporation.

We welcome the opportunity to express our views to the Subcommittee in connection with its studies of the utilization of aerospace technology and manpower, and we want to assure the Subcommittee's members of our continuing interest in this subject and our support of their efforts.

Although we believe that foreseeable changes in government procurement practices will not have an immediate, drastic effect upon either the level of the aerospace industry's business or its manpower requirements, we believe it is wise to continue planning against even a remote possibility that these changes may become more severe than anticipated. Even apart from this consideration, the advantages of speeding the application of aerospace technology to the civilian economy seem to us sufficiently great to warrant a study of the type you are undertaking.

We believe that there are several public and community needs to which aerospace technology could be almost immediately applied and many others to which it could, in varying periods and with varying degrees of supplementation, be made to apply. We believe, further, that such an application would serve to sustain the impetus of our present scientific and technological drive and capture many of its benefits for the civilian economy. Aerospace technology, redirected in part to civilian ends, could aid in the development of new products and industries, assist in the solution of a wide variety of current public problems, and provide, in effect, a new avenue of national growth and new and more satisfying patterns of living.

It is obvious, of course, that in the event of large cutbacks in defense business, such a program would help to maintain aerospace industry strength to meet new defense demands in the future —demands that our experience indicates are very likely to be made again, as they have been so many times in the past. It would provide the basis for a standby industry and technology that could be quickly mobilized to meet possible threats to our security—either those employing existing weapons or those involving technological surprises. To guard against this latter contingency, of course, it is important that a high research and development effort be maintained even during the most apparently tranquil periods. Civilian programs that would sustain this research effort and keep research and development teams together should have a high priority.

We recognize that the application of aerospace research and technological resources to civilian areas of the economy will pose difficult questions regarding the proper roles of government and industry and will require new patterns of government-industry cooperation to achieve social gains without damage to the enterprise system that has been a traditional source of our national strength. Nevertheless, we are hopeful that these new patterns can be further developed. Some of them have already begun to emerge in the government's relationships with the aerospace industry, and it is certainly possible that they can be refined and extended to other than aerospace areas.

In summary, we believe the need is not immediate, since we do not anticipate drastic or sudden reductions in government defense contracting. Nevertheless, we believe it is wise to plan against this contingency. And, even in its absence, we believe the advantages of applying aerospace technology to civilian needs are sufficiently intriguing and compelling to justify this planning.

Following are more specific and detailed comments. We have felt they could be most useful to the Subcommittee if we offered them as answers to what seemed to us four basic questions.

1. *What may be the nature and scope of the manpower problem resulting from possibly changed procurement levels in our industry in the years to come?*

Briefly, we do not believe the prospect for great manpower loss to be as serious as it has been represented to be in some quarters.

Governmental purchases of the things our industry sells—airplanes, missiles, space vehicles, electronics, rocket fuels, instruments, ships, and related services—are now in excess of $20 billion a year. While current defense and space appropriations bills are somewhat under the totals requested by the President, they provide funds to continue this rate of expenditures. Our own forecasts all point to a continued high level of defense and space spending in view of the basic realities of the present world situation.

It seems to us reasonable to expect a nearly constant level of combined defense and space spending over the next few years or, at the most, only a slightly declining one. Recent estimates of a $5 billion decline in defense spending over the next five years appear to us as a valid but perhaps outside figure, more likely subject to downward rather than upward revision. We should think that civilian space spending may hold steady or perhaps increase.

Translated into our own company expectations, future governmental procurement practices should have only a moderate effect upon our company's manpower. Our experience leads us to believe that, if we can continue to maintain our traditional portion of available government business, normal employee turnover plus our regular adaptive measures will help us keep any manpower disruption and dislocation to normal levels.

Of course, it is not simple. Much of our historic turnover occurs among new employees, and very little of it occurs within certain key groups of highly skilled or senior employees. Some dislocations of these latter groups would unquestionably occur. Yet because of past fluctuations in our business, we have a long experience in cushioning dislocations of this type. The normal vicissitudes to which we are constantly exposed in the phasing out of old programs and the buildup of new ones have accustomed us to a certain amount of organizational restructuring and reassignment of personnel.

We are confident that, so long as the decline in defense expenditures is gradual and is accompanied by orderly procurement and contract-termination policies and actions on the part of the government, we can keep manpower disruption to moderate levels. It is the sudden, unexpected, or drastic cutback or cancellation that provides us with a problem we cannot handle in a normal and orderly manner and that is likely to flood the community with large numbers of laid-off employees.

It is worth noting that the problem of this kind of manpower surplus is more likely to be a community than a national one, since even seemingly minor changes in procurement levels or types tend to have profound effects upon single companies or single plants. This is a problem that exists even under conditions of rising government expenditures, as companies fail to obtain particular kinds of new business. It would, of course, be accentuated under declining defense expenditures.

2. *What planning and actions are appropriate and possible for a defense company such as Lockheed in adapting to changed conditions?*

Change has been an outstanding characteristic of our industry from almost the beginning, and our company, as have most others in the industry, has a long experience in anticipating change and adapting to it. The most notable example in recent years is the transition the industry made from the manufacture of airframe to the design and development of missiles and space vehicles and the corresponding transition from an industry of high production to an industry oriented to research, development, and weapon-systems integration and management. We have also, of course, had long experience with changing procurement levels.

To accommodate to these recurring changes in both the levels and types of our business, Lockheed has developed a variety of techniques that have served to cushion the shocks and lessen manpower dislocations—techniques that work well when the changes are gradual and when we are forewarned but are less than adequate in the face of sudden, unannounced, and drastic cutbacks.

These techniques include such things as pre-established orderly transfer, layoff and recall procedures, designed to retain vital skills and longer-service employees. They also include procedures providing for extensive transfer of people from project to project or division to division, and a high degree of support of various manpower-development and training programs that include retraining and conversion-training activities. We encourage the development of a wide variety of skills through employee tuition-reimbursement programs, in-plant training programs, and other educational activities designed to provide a work force of flexible skills and talents.

We also try to anticipate changes and new opportunities through extensive long-range planning and diversification studies. Our development planning group has been making master long-range plans since 1953 and, in these and other ways, tries to help us plot our course as far ahead as ten or twenty years. We believe much of our success in adapting to present-day space and defense needs . . . [arises from] these long-range planning efforts.

On the diversification side, we have also been successful in recent years in extending our competence into new fields through the acquisition of ship-building, propulsion, and electronics companies. Although much of this diversification has been limited to the defense field, we have also developed and marketed a number of nonmilitary products—commercial jet airplanes, flight recorders, fuel-oil registers, bridges, commercial ships, salt-water anticorrosion systems, new metal alloys, airport-fueling services, and many others. . . . [Although] our total sales volume in these areas is relatively small, it represents penetrations into a number of civilian fields where growth potential exists.

Nevertheless, with nearly 96 per cent of our current sales going to U.S. and foreign military customers, we cannot yet claim any great success in diversifying into nongovernmental areas. We believe this is not the result of inadequate foresight or lack of planning but rather reflects the great difficulties that we, in common with other aerospace companies, have in entering commercial fields in spite of our desire to do so and our constant exploration of promising possibilities.

These difficulties stem from a variety of causes. Our industry is technologically oriented toward the very sophisticated product or system involving very high degrees of reliability, quality control, and advanced engineering. Such products, and the techniques and safeguards involved in developing them, are likely to be competitive only in those commercial markets where extremely high-quality and state-of-the-art advances likewise are placed at a high premium.

Then, too, the aerospace industry has little experience in competing for markets in most commercial fields and suffers not only from this inexperience but also from the lack of the kind of organization it needs to compete—extensive dealership organizations, for example, or other commercial outlets for its products.

Behind these problems—problems subject to solution with sufficient time and effort—has lain the persistent inability of the industry to give them the time and attention they require for solution. Our first responsibility has always been to our governmental customers, and we have always felt the strong obligation to devote our best talents and facilities to defense programs, often at the expense of commercial diversification efforts.

Whatever the reasons, the industry has not been notably successful in developing extensive commercial markets, even though it has long recognized the desirability of doing so. Lockheed has made several forays into unrelated commercial fields—aluminum curtain walls, for example—with little success. Other companies have had similar experiences, many of them dating back to the period just after World War II.

All this suggests there is no lack of concern in the industry with establishing commercial markets to balance military ones. It does suggest serious but not insurmountable limitations on the part of aerospace companies to enter many commercial fields under existing conditions.

3. *What can the government do to assist in devising and implementing plans for constructive adjustment to possibly changed procurement levels?*

We believe the government might well consider joining with industry to studying methods of continued employment of defense-industry engineering, scientific, and other manpower resources. We hope that an objective of such studies would be to insure the retention of technological-team competence against the time that it might again be needed for rapid conversion back to future defense work. And we would urge that the research and development sector of the industry be permitted to continue to devote a major share of its attention to defense problems even under the most stringent cutbacks in order to maintain its ability to cope with new technological threats to our security. Experience proves that the finest research results are obtained when a strong and continuing level of effort is maintained.

We, therefore, look with favor on such efforts as that contemplated in the recent bill Mr. Hart and Mr. Humphrey introduced before the Senate to establish a commission on the application of advanced technology to community and manpower needs and are glad to observe that this bill provides for an advisory panel to include representatives of government, private industry, and educational, and technological institutions.

We believe this kind of approach may prove a valuable supplement to tax-cutting measures . . . [because] it will have the effect of preserving defense competence while partially directing it into other useful areas. It can also be pinpointed to specific community needs in ways that tax cuts cannot.

4. *What other areas of activity show promise for utilization of the defense industry's technological resources?*

As part of our own company's present long-range planning, we are now conducting a study of broad areas of national, community, and human needs that might be served by the application of our own company's technology. For the most part, private enterprise has not yet undertaken these tasks, largely because they are marginally uneconomic in our present state of development. Many of them are very large in scope. They represent potential areas of promise to the aerospace industry as a whole because they can make use of existing aerospace technological and productive skills, because they will benefit from the application of aerospace research resources, or because they involve the extensive systems-engineering ability that is to be found within the industry.

We have not yet completed this study, and the following list is incomplete and certainly not definitive. But it will serve, we hope, to suggest some of the kinds of areas in which the broad competences of the industry might beneficially be employed under conditions that would make this employment economically feasible. These conditions would probably require varying degrees of government support, until the programs become economically self-sustaining.

The following projects or programs may well serve as examples of commercial areas in which aerospace technology, with varying degrees of conversion effort, might be applied:

1. *Supersonic transport.* This, of course, is a current project for which Lockheed is now competing. It is mentioned here merely to identify it as a type of peacetime conversion effort that is already underway and that may be regarded as setting a precedent.

2. *Transport helicopters.* The short-haul use of helicopters can be greatly expanded, particularly in areas of high-density population. New helicopter developments, some of them within our own company, are producing more efficient and more economical vehicles. Concentrated effort in this field, as well as in the whole area of vertical take-off and landing craft, could produce substantial transportation improvements.

3. *Facilities for general aviation.* These involve such items as improved communication and navigation aids, cargo-handling devices, air-traffic-control systems, more and better terminal facilities, and so on, all contributing to the ease and safety of flying and stimulating commercial air travel and private flying alike.

4. *Integrated transportation systems.* These are vast systems-engineering projects involving the coordination of rail, road, air, and even sea facilities to avoid duplication and expedite travel. Perhaps one way to visualize such a system is through the concept of an integrated terminal, fed locally by rail, bus, or private automobiles arriving at different levels; fed from medium distances by helicopters, feeder planes, bus, or rail service; and fed from larger distances by subsonic or supersonic transports and ultimately, perhaps, even rocket-powered aircraft.

5. *Satellite programs.* This is an area already under exploitation for civilian ends by NASA [National Aeronautics and Space Administration] and, in the case of the communications satellite, by private enterprise. The utility of the communications satellite in relaying voice, video, or pulse information is well-known. Other satellite projects offer similar advantages. Weather satellites, for example, can furnish large national benefits in the accurate prediction, and possibly even control, of weather. Greater emphasis on these practical satellite programs is worth considering.

6. *Harbor development.* This area may have more application to our own company than to others in the industry because of the construction, dredging, and other skills of our ship-building subsidiary. However, we see it as a possible outlet for our capability, particularly in connection with the project following.

7. *Merchant-marine improvement.* American ships and the shipping industry may be substantially benefitted by application of aerospace technology. New types of high-speed vehicles with which we are now experimenting include hydrofoil craft and interface vehicles that skim above the water. Anticorrosion systems, protective coatings, and cargo-containerization systems are already under development or being produced by Lockheed with the expectation that the number of commercial marine products can be extended in the future. In addition, we are currently expanding our ship-building facilities to permit the construction of large commercial ocean-going vessels.

8. *Underwater systems.* This is a field whose potential is still largely unknown. For the past several years, Lockheed has supported an oceanographic research program which includes the operation of a fully equipped oceangoing research vessel. Our present investigation of underwater mining and exploration is but one outgrowth of this research effort.

9. *Air-pollution control devices.* The importance of air-pollution control to public health and welfare needs no comment. This is a large-scale project requiring intensive research efforts and perhaps developing into large hardware production programs. Aerospace technology is engaged in a portion of this area now in connection with investigation of closed ecological systems for space travel.

10. *Water-conservation systems.* Integrated water systems involve dams, pipelines, antipollution treatment, and so on. They are of

particular interest to our company because they make use of our heavy construction experience.

11. *Waste-disposal systems.* These systems could provide more efficient collection and disposal methods than currently in use, perhaps with recapture of waste products. Lockheed already has some experience in this area, involving construction of a pilot plant to convert waste materials into economically useful gases and solid products such as soil conditioners.

12. *Automated-materials-handling systems.* There are many systems of modern living, such as hospitals, warehousing, and consumer food distribution, in which the extensive or inefficient use of human labor suggests room for improvement through electro-mechanical handling systems and automatic controls.

13. *Power conversion and storage.* The industry has long been exploring new and unusual sources of power for space propulsion and auxiliary power supply to spacecraft. Of particular commercial interest is the fuel cell, still under development, that converts chemical to electrical power directly and may serve a number of highly useful purposes in the future, possibly even to the extent of replacing the gasoline engine.

14. *Nuclear electric power.* Already competitive in some areas of the world, nuclear power should become even more widespread in the future with the development of reactors capable of producing lower-cost power, and with the development of fast breeder reactors, and ultimately through the control of thermonuclear reaction. Small nuclear reactors for marine and space propulsion, long-endurance space power sources, and remote site operations represent an area where continuing research efforts will be needed. Many aerospace companies maintain a nuclear capability that can be put to work to speed this process. Our own company operates a nuclear research laboratory that does radiation studies, and builds training reactors and radioisotope power sources.

15. *Information systems.* The industry's high competence in advanced military electronic systems offers great potential for the future development of commercial information systems of various kinds. These range from large command and control systems (air-traffic control is a familiar example) through various data storage and retrieval systems (automated libraries, medical information systems, and so on) to smaller management information systems

or business systems for industry. Indeed, it can be stated that the growth and vitality of the nation's commercial electronics industry owe much to past military electronics research and development efforts. And current studies underway in the areas of microminiaturization and high-reliability components will be of great benefit to commercial users in the not-too-distant future.

16. *Salt-water conversion.* Perhaps the ultimate answer to the nation's needs for water, salt-water conversion, although not directly related to present aerospace research efforts, offers such positive public and community benefits that it might well warrant a major attack by aerospace research and technical teams.

Aerospace companies today have a widespread research competence ranging over most of the physical and mathematical sciences and many of the life sciences. They have, in fact, the highest research and scientific competence to be found anywhere in the nation and represent our chief reservoir of assembled scientific talent. When you add to this the industry's high proportion of skilled labor, its productive abilities and facilities, and its outstanding systems-engineering skill, it appears to be ideally suited to create and develop massive engineering programs that can add greatly to the public good.

To some, programs such as those listed above may appear visionary. Perhaps they are. But on reflection it is possible they may be no more so than was the concept of the earth satellite ten years ago. To insure constructive planning and selection of such ventures, each will need careful appraisal, balancing considerations of technical feasibility, economic practicality, and usefulness in meeting the nation's public and community needs. We are confident, however, that among these and other programs and projects there exist opportunities in which the scientific and engineering resources of defense industries may be directed effectively, at the same time mitigating the consequences of possible future cutbacks in defense production.

THE REGIONAL IMPACT OF DEFENSE EXPENDITURES: ITS MEASUREMENT AND PROBLEMS OF ADJUSTMENT

Charles M. Tiebout

Charles M. Tiebout is Professor of Economics at the University of Washington. He has written extensively on theoretical and empirical aspects of regional economics. This paper discusses the relative dependence of certain regions in the United States on defense demand, and the structural problems of adjustment posed for such regions by large defense cutbacks. The essay is especially valuable for its discussion of just how such "dependence" should be measured and for the empirical results summarized. It was originally presented as a statement to the Subcommittee on Employment and Manpower of the U.S. Senate Committee on Labor and Public Welfare in November 1963. It is reprinted here by permission of Charles M. Tiebout. (Printed in Nation's Manpower Revolution, Hearings, Part 7. [Washington, D.C.: USGPO, 1963], pp. 2516-23.) *Some deletions have been made with the author's permission.*

This paper[1] takes on a threefold task: (1) To show why defense expenditures may be more significant as a source of regional or community income and employment than is generally appreciated; (2) to suggest the order of magnitude of this impact on certain communities and, at the same time, [to] point out how the impact can be measured; and (3) to consider some of the difficulties attendant on shifts in these expenditures. The conclusion will be that for some regions and communities it is a most important source of income and employment, the impact is measurable without extensive research costs, and that the regional aspect presents a nasty set of problems when offsets to changes in the over-all level of defense spending are considered.

THE ROLE OF DEFENSE EXPENDITURES
IN THE COMMUNITY INCOME STREAM

It is rather self-evident that some regions or communities have declined because they lost their "export base"—i.e., the ability to sell their products to other regions of the nation. The decline of the coal export to other regions is an important factor in the West Virginia situation; loss of ore and forest products markets has hurt the Upper Peninsula of Michigan; and textile plant closings have removed the export base of a number of New England communities. Thus, the export-base concept, where the term *exports* means sales to other regions as well as international trade, serves as a useful tool in explaining changes in the over-all level of income and employment in communities and regions. It is a recognition of this fact which has prodded many states, community civic groups, and others into efforts to attract industries.

Recognition of this concept does not imply that all of a region's growth must be generated from its export market. Increases in local productivity [do] indeed take place. Moreover, this concept does not really tell us much about regional differences in per capita income. Yet, it is a valuable tool for understanding why some regions grow and others decline in terms of total employment, total income, and population.

What does this export-base concept have to do with defense expenditures? From a regional or community viewpoint, defense sales are part of this export market. The effect on the local economy is the same as other export sales. A Boeing 707 jet ordered by MATS [Military Air Transport Service] has about the same impact on Seattle as one ordered by American Airlines. Thus, it is useful to think of sales to defense in the same way one considers a region's export market.

The necessity for identifying this defense market separately is that it has an impact on total income and employment seemingly out of proportion to its share of total income and employment. Some 450,000 people in the State of California worked for the [U.S.] Department of Defense (DOD) or, as was true for more than 90 per cent, for firms whose sales went to the DOD.[2] Of these, about three fourths—some 290,000—were employed in manufacturing. These figures, taken in conjunction with total employment in California, do not loom as terribly large. Total employment in this period was some 5.9 million. Seemingly, the defense market amounts to just about 8 per cent of total employment. Is this the total impact?

By no means, for these figures show only the direct impact on employment. The direct impact measures those jobs resulting from direct sales to defense. The indirect impact on the region must also be included. For the indirect impact measures the employment generated by subcontractors and other suppliers and, in turn, their suppliers. Ten thousand persons employed on the final assembly of a military aircraft may mean another 5000 are employed in airframe construction, which, in turn, may have required 500 employees in the metal fabricating industry—which, in turn, may mean 200 employees in the metals industry. And, of course, this only illustrates the indirect impact on some other industries. In reality, it is even more complicated and many industries are involved.

Turning back to the California figures, when this indirect employment impact is also included, total employment serving the defense market rises from some 450,000 to some 710,000 employees, or an increase of 260,000 employees.[3] Instead of accounting for only some 8 per cent of total employment, almost 12 per cent is involved; yet, this is not the end of the impact by any means.

The induced impact on the region also should be included. The induced impact has several components: the consumer-induced impact, the business-induced impact, and the local-government-induced impact.

As a result of the income and employment generated directly and indirectly via defense expenditures in the region, consumer total income will rise. In turn, part of this will be spent in the region on retail goods, services, housing, and other consumer items. This will create additional income and employment in the area as the familiar induced expansion takes place.

In like manner, business firms will need to invest to expand output to satisfy the demands created by both the direct, indirect, and induced effects.

Finally, local governments will need to spend, both on current and capital items, in order to accommodate the population's needs.

If these effects are taken into account, the California picture is

quite different. Instead of some 710,000 employees tied directly
and indirectly to the defense market, the total impact of defense
expenditures rises to around 2.6 million employees or somewhat
more than 40 per cent of total employment.

Naturally, this is only an estimate and involved certain assumptions about consumer, business, and government behavior. Yet, the
fact that it is a large percent[age] of total employment should not
be a surprise. After all, history does report that, in spite of the
number of retail merchants, saloonkeepers, blacksmiths, and so
forth who may have been in business, towns that lost the gold-
mine export base became ghost towns. The gold export market
impact—direct, indirect, and induced—accounted for 100 per cent
of total employment.

The illustration of the gold-mine ghost town should not be mis-
understood. To suggest that over 40 per cent of California's employment is related to defense expenditures does not mean a complete cutback in defense spending would result in a loss of almost
half of the jobs. Offsets in the form of the development of other
products and services can take place, as will be discussed below.
These data only suggest that this could be the magnitude of the
impact in the absence of any offsets at all.

Summarizing the economic impact of defense spending in regions,
be they smaller communities or statewide regions: sales to the
defense market are part of a region's export-to-other-regions base.
These sales not only generate direct income and employment, but
indirect income and employment in other industries in the process
of buying needed inputs. Further, as a result of greater income
and employment, induced demands for consumer goods, business
investment, and local government services also arise, creating even
more income and employment.

This measurement of the impact of defense expenditures on a
region does not, of course, account for the full economic impact.
Defense-oriented regions may have different skill mixes in their
labor force, the types and attitudes of unions may differ and other
characteristics may reflect a defense orientation. The impact measurement discussed above does not account for this type of impact.
. . . [Although] these may be important, they are left to other
frameworks and studies.

IMPACT MEASUREMENT

It is one thing to spell out the various components of the impact of defense spending on a community, but the actual measurement is another problem. The most difficult problem comes at the subcontract level and even more remote stages of production, above classified as the indirect level.

The problem that arises can be simply illustrated by reference to two hypothetical communities, which for convenience, we will call "Primetown" and "Subville." Primetown may appear to be heavily involved in the defense effort as known prime contracts are let to firms in the community. Subville, however, may receive no prime contracts at all. Yet, it may be more heavily involved in the defense industry. This could happen for the well-known reason that the place of a prime contract award may not be the actual spot where the work is done. Subville may be a large area for subcontracts or other inputs needed in the production process.

The reason that this is a problem is that Primetown may think it is more heavily involved in the defense industry than is actually the case. Even worse, Subville may not realize its commitment to this market. Unfortunately, until both the direct and indirect impacts are measured, the induced impact cannot be estimated. Thus, the problem of measuring the impact is of more than academic interest.

There are several techniques useful in getting at the regional impact: (1) trace out the contracts from prime to subs and on down the line; (2) spell out the interindustry relations; and (3) work from the bottom up. Each of these has certain advantages and disadvantages, as will be seen.

Tracing out the impact from prime to subs has a certain amount of appeal. The data developed by Isard and Ganschow are helpful in identifying the regional impact of prime contracts.[4] For specific programs, other sources can provide the starting place. The next step is to go from the primes to the subs, perhaps by surveys. It is also necessary to note the location of the subcontractors. Further analysis of the subcontractors can pick up the second tier of subcontracting and so on. Eventually, things get pretty messy as diffusion takes place.

The major difficulty with this approach is that it does not account for enough of the impact. It may appear that if 50 per cent of a prime is subcontracted, tracing out two layers of subcontracting will account for 87.5 per cent of the impact—50 per cent plus 50 per cent of 50 per cent (25 per cent) plus 50 per cent of 25 per cent (12.5 per cent). This is not the case. A prime who sub-contracts 50 per cent does not produce the remaining 50 per cent himself; i.e., the remainder is not all value added by the prime. Other inputs along with those officially "subcontracted" will be purchased, and these are part of the indirect impact. Hence, less is accounted for than appears at first glance.

The second or interindustry-relations approach works from both the top down and [from] the bottom up. The technique is known as interregional input-output analysis. The mechanics are not appropriate to this discussion, but the results of such an approach are of interest. Essentially, the sales of materials and services from one industry to another are traced out both within a region and between regions. Thus, steel from Pittsburgh may go to a fabricator in Cleveland, to an electrical-component manufacturer in Chicago, and on to an aircraft assembler in Los Angeles. Given the data in sufficient detail, all this can be traced out.

. . . [Although] this is desirable, data difficulties make this approach more of a conceptual ideal than an operating reality. The data do not exist and can be generated only with considerable research effort.

The third, or bottom-up, approach appears more promising and has been used in two forms. One variant has been to determine, via surveys, where firms sell their outputs. How much is sold to such markets as the federal government, local consumers, and other industries in the area. This has been reported elsewhere.[5]

The second variant to the bottom-up approach is quite simple: survey firms asking three questions: (1) What percent[age] do you sell directly to DOD? (2) Considering all other sales, what percent[age] went to known prime and subcontractors? (3) Finally, considering all other sales not accounted for by (1) and (2), what percent[age] of these ended up in products sold to DOD?

Although the particular study referred to in examining the results of such an approach also includes NASA [National Aeronautics and Space Administration], this accounts for a relatively small portion of the total.[6] . . . [Although] this particular approach is a short-cut, the results seem quite reasonable when compared to other available information. Its advantage lies in the small research cost involved.

SOME IMPACT ESTIMATES

Some studies have been carried out in an effort to measure this impact, although sometimes it is only a byproduct. For the information of the committee, these results are summarized. In the short time available, it has not been possible to make an exhaustive survey of impact studies.

The two tables presented below summarize the results of two separate studies in California. The Los Angeles-Long Beach SMSA (Standard Metropolitan Statistical Area) employment generated by defense expenditures is shown in Table 1. Only some 7.7 per cent of the employment is directly tied to defense-space. (In this and in the other material on San Francisco, it was possible to separate NASA expenditures from defense spending. However, the available data suggest that this is only a very small portion of the total.) When indirect employment is added, an additional 7.9 per cent of the labor force is involved. Thus, the total direct and indirect effects, as these terms are defined above, account for over 15 per cent of total employment. If the induced effects are added, the total impact swells to 43.5 per cent of total employment.* Although caution must be used in interpreting these data, it is safe to suggest that Los Angeles is a defense-space-oriented economy—and strongly so.

The San Francisco area is another story. Table 2 provides the same information for the Bay Area. Two words of caution: the metropolitan area, as defined, does not include Santa Clara County, which is a site for defense production, and the study from which these data are taken has a downward bias which understates the indirect sales to defense-space—as noted in Footnote † accompanying the table.

In spite of a downward bias some 15.9 per cent of the area's

---

* In this and the two tables that follow, the totals summing from above do not add up to 100 per cent. The residual represents the employment generated by other markets.

total employment is defense-space generated. Much of the direct employment is in the nonmanufacturing industries and is explained by the presence of military establishments, headquarters offices, and research centers located in the bay area. . . .

A somewhat hurry-up study of the Seattle SMSA yields the results shown in Table 3. These estimates are only rough and the data are drawn from a variety of sources. Nevertheless, the results are of interest. In terms of defense-space orientation, the area is less heavily committed than Los Angeles, with some 42.2 per cent of the employment related to defense spending. Obviously much of this reflects the activity of Boeing Company. As such, the propor-

Table 1

Defense-Space Generated Employment (Direct, Indirect, and Induced)
Los Angeles-Long Beach, SMSA: *1960**

	Employment	Percent[age] of Total Employment
Direct defense-space	204,800	7.7
Indirect defense-space	209,800	7.9
Induced defense-space	738,000	27.8
Via consumption**	469,000	17.6
Via housing investment**	69,000	2.6
Via business investment**	58,000	2.2
Via local government**	142,000	5.4
Total defense-space generated	1,152,700	43.5
Total employment†	2,649,000	100.0

* Employment data shown are average employment for the year 1959. However, the percent[age] allocations were made on the basis of surveys of sales during 1960. See W. Lee Hansen and Charles M. Tiebout, "An Intersectoral Flows Analysis of the California Economy," *Review of Economics and Statistics,* XLV (November 1963).

** Estimated from Hansen and Tiebout, *op. cit.*

† This estimate of employment was made for the Hansen-Tiebout study. It includes agricultural and self-employed persons. Hence, it is higher than the usual figures reported for total employment.

tion in defense-space will vary as that firm's Seattle operations move back and forth from military to commercial production.

PECULIAR PROBLEMS OF ADJUSTMENT

The above data suggest the peculiar problem associated with shifts in defense expenditures: the impact is not uniform throughout the various regions of the nation. Indeed, it is rather concentrated. Shifts in the form of cutbacks will hit some areas harder than others. Offset programs, such as induced consumer spending made possible by tax reductions, are general in impact. Specific

Table 2

Defense-Space Generated Employment (Direct, Indirect, and Induced),
*San Francisco-Oakland, SMSA: 1960 ** *

	Employment	Percent[age] of Total Employment
Direct defense-space	51,300	4.6
Indirect defense-space	10,100	.9
Induced defense-space	116,000	10.5
Via consumption**	72,300	6.5
Via housing investment**	11,200	1.0
Via business investment**	5,100	.5
Via local government**	27,400	2.5
Total defense-space generated	177,400	15.9
Total employment†	1,113,500	100.0

* Employment data shown are average employment for the year 1959. However, the percent[age] allocations were made on the basis of surveys of sales during 1960. See W. Lee Hansen and Charles M. Tiebout, "An Intersectoral Flows Analysis of the California Economy," *Review of Economics and Statistics,* XLV (November 1963).
** Estimated from Hansen and Tiebout, *op. cit.*
† This estimate of employment was made for the Hansen-Tiebout study. It includes agricultural and self-employed persons. Hence, it is higher than the usual figures reported for total employment.

Table 3

Defense-Space Generated Employment (Direct, Indirect, and Induced),
Seattle, SMSA: 1962

	Employment	Percent[age] of Total Employment
Direct defense-space	55,800	11.8
Indirect defense-space	16,200	3.4
Induced defense-space	127,900	27.0
Total defense-space generated	199,900	42.2
Total employment	473,600	100.0

Sources: Estimated from variety of sources, including published information from state agencies; newspaper clippings; Walter Isard and James Ganschow, Awards of Prime Military Contracts by County, State, and Metropolitan Area of the United States, Fiscal Year 1962 (Philadelphia: Regional Science Research Institute); and other such sources of information.

federal programs, which might be desired, with less expenditures needed for defense, are also nationwide in scope and not particular to the regions hard-hit by defense cutbacks.

It might be suggested that this is merely a problem of the mobility of labor. If certain regions decline and other regions grow, no loss is involved. After all, immediately after World War II, this nation had a tremendous reshuffling of population away from war-production centers such as Bremerton, Wash[ington], and New London, Conn[ecticut]. All this was accomplished without much sacrifice. Hence, why worry about a reshuffle away from regions such as California?

There is, however, a big difference between post-World War II experience and possible shifts resulting from cutbacks in today's defense expenditures. Large movements from these regions will be accompanied by substantial losses in investment these people have made in their houses, land, educational systems, and other local investments. This was not true after World War II. People knew it [i.e., the war] was a short-run situation and few long-term investment commitments were made or could have been made because of wartime shortages. This is not the case today. Millions of people have made investments in houses over almost a two-decade period in places such as Los Angeles and Seattle. Even disregarding . . . [the] fact that many people who once lived elsewhere prefer to live in these areas, the dollar loss could be staggering.

The main point of these remarks should be quite clear: aggregative statements which ignore the regional component of defense reduction offset programs can be very misleading.

For particular communities, shifts brought about by the changing patterns of defense spending may impose an additional loss over and above that brought about by the loss of part of its export base. The evidence does suggest that skill and the education level associated with this activity are quite high. Thus, communities may lose a valuable source of intellectual, educational, and business leadership.

In addition, the defense-oriented industries have been a source of new entrepreneurs who start new businesses. Not all of these spin off to serve the defense market. Some produce new consumer and business goods and services.

The problem here is that these individuals in their roles as potential entrepreneurs cannot be turned on like a faucet. They start new activities at the "appropriate" time. Hence, they cannot be expected to fill the void left by a regional dropoff in the defense-serving industries. Instead, a good many can be expected to leave the region.

Not only may the people in defense-oriented areas have different skills, but the firms do as well. Many of these firms are not used to dealing with the nongovernmental market, except as sellers of aircraft. Hence, the shift to a consumer or business market might be more difficult for these firms than . . . [for those that] already have considerable experience in the consumer and business market.

Beyond this, there does not seem to be any major difference between the drop in defense impact on a community and any other kind of export-markets loss.

OFFSET PROGRAMS: FEDERAL, STATE, AND LOCAL

When the proverbial chips are down, the real question is: What does one do to offset or soften the blow or shifts on a community? What steps can be taken by the local area, the state, and the federal government? Here the comfortable world of research must, in part, give way to some speculation and value judgments. And, of course, no easy or simple answers pop out.

Probably the first question is: Who is responsible for offsetting action? Even this is not obvious. Insofar as people invested in these regions on some kind of expectation of permanency of the defense-effort level, certainly there is a federal responsibility. There are ample precedents of federal assumption of responsibility where regions have suffered from market changes in which federal actions were hardly responsible. The Area Redevelopment Act is a prime example of federal responsibility, where the main effort has been to bring jobs to people in distressed regions. The various agricultural-support programs also have a strong regional element, even if they are not explicitly designed as regional programs.

At the same time, states and localities also have a responsibility. For one thing, without acceptance of some responsibility on their part, there may be little the federal government can do. Again, this is the kind of shared responsibility as put forth in the Area Redevelopment Act. Again, as in the Area Redevelopment Act, major responsibility lies with the federal government because it is the only unit large enough to be effective.

The first step in preparing for such shifts is to recognize them. It does not seem amiss to suggest many communities do not recognize the importance of this market to their community. In part this reflects a natural reluctance to admit anything might be all but rosy. Yet, even more fundamental, the impact is more subtle than [it] appears. . . . This is because the major part of the impact is indirect or induced, as noted above.

It seems highly desirable to sponsor, perhaps by the federal government in connection with other programs, studies to determine the impact of defense on the communities of the nation. As noted above, these need not be terribly costly. This might provide the "shock" effect needed to bring about serious consideration of possible offset programs.

The next task is the hardest. Suppose a community finds out it is heavily involved in the defense effort. What steps can it take now to offset such changes as might take place?

A few nonsense or near-nonsense steps should be avoided. Calls for "diversification," "attracting industry," "promoting shop-at-home campaigns," and the like are largely a waste of effort. These represent the growing pains of regional economic-development programs. It is useful to recall two facts of U.S. economic life: (1) manufacturing employment in the United States has not risen in the past decade; and (2) in most regions the major employers are firms . . . [which] started in the area and not ones which were enticed into the region.

This does not mean that promotional efforts are not desirable. It only serves to remind us that not too much should be expected from this approach.

A more positive and promising approach would be to start by asking a question other than: How can we get a larger share of the U.S. economic pie? Instead, it seems more fruitful to ask: How can we make the pie bigger? In other words, forget about getting outside industry into the region and concentrate on development from within. A rather simple rule of thumb might be to ask if any action will increase U.S. net growth or merely redistribute regionally what would have taken place anyhow. If it is the latter, drop it. Probably it will not work anyhow.

Thus, we come to the nub of the question: What positive steps can be taken? The main goal is to promote new local firms or to help existing ones to expand. Here, three general steps are suggested which lead to consideration of a possible federal program.

One fruitful step would be the consideration of Worcester-type programs. In the late 1940s, [the] Worcester, Mass[achusetts] Chamber of Commerce inaugurated a program of aid to local small business. Four experts were hired by the local Chamber: an accountant, a production expert, a transportation specialist, and a sales engineer.* These people were available free to small business in the area and actually called on firms to be of continuing help. Unfortunately, the program was discontinued for reasons which are not known to the writer.

Such a program seems eminently worthwhile. Many small firms need and can profit by this kind of continuing help in their early formative years. Moreover, knowledge that such aid is available should be a spur to others to enter business for themselves.

* This discussion is from memory and may . . . [err] in some of the details. Regrettably, with all the research in the area of development, this writer knows of no history of this program.

A second possibility would be to set up new business-research buildings. This idea should not be confused with the shell building approach.

Shell industrial buildings have been put up by local industrial groups in the hope of attracting industry. At times these are offered at low or free rent. Not all of these programs, it should be noted, have been smashingly successful.

Instead of a shell building, it would be desirable to build an adaptable industrial plant, perhaps of a few hundred thousand square feet. The building could be partitioned into smaller units from, say, 1000 feet on up. This facility could be made available at no rent or a modest rent for new firms set up by local people. Not all of these would be expected to be successful, and no doubt some would fail.

The problem this approach attacks is the one of credit for new ventures. In spite of many attempts, most efforts to aid small business have become conservative in their lending collateral requirements and do not get at the problem. Such a step would at least remove one barrier to entry.

A third step is even less definite. As a college professor with some exposure to business schools, . . . [I venture] an observation: business schools seem to do little to encourage students to go out on their own in business. National and local firms often recruit some of the most able talent. . . . [Although] nobody wants to deny them this opportunity, it does seem that some thought might be given to encouraging students to go out on their own. This is the time in their lives when the cost of failure, if it occurs, would be small. Further, the evidence does suggest that failure is not considered a black mark to blight a person's career. . . . [Although] no specific steps are suggested here, this topic is tossed in for exploration.

It may be that some of these suggestions, if they are considered worthwhile, can be carried out within existing federal programs. If not, it may be desirable to consider a Business Opportunities Act. Such an Act would not only allow for planning for possible reconversion, but could also carry out specific programs along the lines suggested here.

Finally, it may not be inappropriate to suggest that the time to plan is now. . . . [Although] solutions may not be easy, the desirability of disarmament should not be mitigated against because of regional interests.

NOTES

1. This paper was prepared on rather short notice. Hence I have borrowed from other works rather extensively. The three major sources are: W. Lee Hansen and Charles M. Tiebout, "An Intersectoral Flows Analysis of the California Economy," *Review of Economics and Statistics,* XLV (November 1963), and the references cited therein; Richard Peterson and Charles M. Tiebout, "Defense-Space Expenditures: Their Local and Spatial Repercussions," a paper presented at the American Economic Association joint with the Regional Science Association, Boston, Mass., December 1963; and Charles M. Tiebout, *The Community Economic-Base Study,* Committee for Economic Development, Supplementary Paper No. 16, December 1962.

2. Estimated from Hansen and Tiebout, *op. cit.*

3. Estimated from Hansen and Tiebout, *op. cit.,* and Peterson and Tiebout, *op. cit.*

4. Walter Isard and James Ganschow, *Awards of Prime Military Contracts by County, State, and Metropolitan Area of the United States, Fiscal Year 1960* (Philadelphia: Regional Science Research Institute).

5. See Hansen and Tiebout, *op. cit.*

6. Peterson and Tiebout, *op. cit.*

THE IMPACT OF ARMS REDUCTION
ON RESEARCH AND DEVELOPMENT

Richard R. Nelson

*Richard Nelson has written considerably on the economic aspects
of research and development, including its interrelationships with
defense expenditures. He was formerly a member of the staff of
the President's Council of Economic Advisers, and was also a member of the Panel on Economic Impacts of Disarmament for the U.S.
Arms Control and Disarmament Agency. He is currently on the
staff of The RAND Corporation. The following article first appeared
in the* American Economic Review, *Vol. 53, May 1963, pp. 435-446.
Copyright © 1963, by American Economic Association; reprinted
by permission of the American Economic Association and Richard
R. Nelson. A few deletions and changes have been made with the
permission of the author.*

INTRODUCTION *

WHY ARE WE CONCERNED?

It is not just a coincidence that the 1950s, which were marked
by the largest peacetime military budgets in American history,
also were marked by a striking rise in the percentage of our economic resources allocated to scientific research and development.
Indeed there are tight links between these two phenomena running
both ways.

Somewhere in the neighborhood of 15 per cent of our defense
outlays are for research and development . . . , and somewhere

* The research which led to this paper was financed by the Research Program on Economic Adjustments to Disarmament.

between 50 per cent and 60 per cent of our total research and development expenditures is financed by defense agencies.** Although these measures are crude, it is clear that our defense expenditure has had a very major impact on the magnitude and allocation of our research and development effort.

Looking at the matter the other way around, our post-World War II history of no major central war between the two big power blocs and, at the same time, extremely high levels of peacetime military expenditure must be attributed, in large part, to research and development. Modern science has created a world in which both the potential devastation to an aggressor against a well-prepared adversary, and the costs required to be well prepared, are unprecedented. It is modern science which lies behind both the balance and the delicateness of the delicate balance of terror.

It is clear that significant arms reduction would have a major impact on the size and allocation of our research and development effort. Why should this be of concern? There are two conceptually distinct reasons. One is the familiar problem of frictional unemployment. The second is rather special and is related to the nature and role of research and development in a basically free-enterprise economy. Research and development is an activity yielding a large crop of external economies. A significant cutback in research and development could retard the rate of technological progress in our economy and might present a socially undesirable reallocation of resources. This point will be elaborated—and qualified significantly—later.

MEASURING THE RESEARCH AND DEVELOPMENT IMPACT OF DEFENSE

Anyone who thinks it an easy matter to separate military from nonmilitary research and development should try it. Civilian uses of electronic and other equipment developed for military purposes are numerous and important, and, on the other hand, much of our military equipment incorporates hosts of devices, materials, processes, designs, and concepts not originally conceived or de-

* * In this paper, defense *research and development* is defined to include the programs of the U.S. Department of Defense and the military programs of the Atomic Energy Commission. NASA [National Aeronautics and Space Administration] work is not included.

veloped for military purposes. In research, it is difficult to think of many areas of physics or mathematics where the results of really significant breakthroughs would not affect both civilian and military technology; and nowadays many areas of genetics, medicine, and even geology may have important military applications.*

The fact that many research areas and many development projects may have both military and civilian applications leads to several difficult problems in measuring the impact of our defense effort on research and development. One problem is that defense support of research often is a substitute for, not an addition to, nondefense support. For example, a good deal of the work in space technology financed by the [U.S.] Department of Defense (. . . DOD) would probably be picked up by NASA if the DOD stopped its support, and similarly if NASA closed down, a good part of its work would almost certainly be financed by the DOD. Much of the work undertaken in private industrial labs on semiconductor devices would be financed by the companies themselves if DOD support was withdrawn, and the DOD might well kick more into the kitty if the companies cut back on their own financing.**

The "substitution" problem tends to make research and development spending by the DOD overstate the real impact of defense on research and development. The "accounting" problem tends the opposite way. To understand the accounting problem, assume that a $4 billion defense contract has been let with a major aircraft company for the design, development, and procurement of a new ballistic missile. Assume that $1 billion of the contract are especially labeled "research and development"; and thus appear on the [National Science Foundation] (NSF) accounts as "defense" research and development.† But much of the work on the contract will be subcontracted out, and though much of this subcontracting work may involve considerable research and development on components, research and development work done by subcontractors

---

* See, for example, Striner, Sherman and Karadbil, *Defense Spending and the U.S. Economy* (Baltimore: Operations Research Office, Johns Hopkins University, 1959).

** The history of the synthetic rubber industry testifies to the importance of this substitution effect. See Robert Solo, "Research and Development in the Synthetic Rubber Industry," *Quarterly Journal of Economics,* 1954.

† The NSF calculates that the total government contribution was about $9 billion. It is estimated that between 75 and 80 per cent of this is military.

may or may not be accounted under the $1 billion figure. It is if the prime contractor allots part of the research and development contract to subcontractors. But when the prime contractor has an option to shop around to find the best components and possible subcontractors compete with each other to provide the best component design or prototype, the research and development work is done on the potential subcontractor's own financing. When a firm gains the subcontract, the terms of the formal contract are for delivery of hardware. The research and development expense is covered in the contract sum, but in the DOD's books this is hardware outlay, and in the NSF's books this is privately financed research and development. With the materials, subsubcomponents, and other inputs to the weapon system well down at the base of the assembly pyramid, the story is similar. And to get all of the research and development associated with the $4 billion weapon-system contract, we must trace our way back through the entire input-output matrix, attempting to estimate the induced research and development outlays of the firms supplying the subcontractors, the firms supplying these firms, and so on.

A third problem of measuring the impact relates to the effect of rising demand upon supply. To the extent that net defense demand for research and development has been positive, there probably has been some induced increase both in the number of students who take training in the sciences and engineering and in the per-cent[age] of these people who have such training who work in research and development. In addition, the defense research and development programs have had a quite noticeable effect on the type of science and engineering training graduate students and undergraduates take.

Despite these difficulties, in this paper the spending of the DOD and the [Atomic Energy Commission] (AEC) in defense programs will be used as the measure of defense-related research and development.

A Simple Linear Model

THE NAÏVE MODEL

For present purposes, we are interested in the impact of certain specified reductions in defense spending upon research and development. For convenience, we shall take as reference a 50 per cent cutback in defense spending, but all results will be in terms of any cutback in defense spending. In order to set an upper bound on the impact, in this section it will be assumed that the cutback is all at once; in a later section, this assumption will be relaxed.

The model rests on the assumption that the ratio of defense research and development to defense final demand can be treated as a constant, as can the ratio of nondefense research and development to nondefense final demand. These constants can be used to estimate what might happen to research and development expenditures when demand shifts from defense to nondefense. We shall assume that appropriate fiscal and monetary policy assures that all declines in defense final demand are compensated for by equal dollar increases in civilian final demand.

In 1960, about $14 billion of our economy's resources were spent on research and development. The . . . [DOD] and the military part of the [AEC] supported somewhere around $7 billion of this work. Total 1960 defense expenditure was about $45 billion, including some of the AEC's work, and thus defense research and development was between 15 and 16 per cent of defense final demand. . . . [Because the GNP] for 1960 was about $500 billion, nondefense research and development represented about 1.5 per cent of nondefense final demand. If these ratios stay constant, a dollar reduction in military final demand compensated by a dollar increase in civilian demand would result in a 14 cent reduction in total research and development. Cutting the military budget in half and increasing civilian demand to compensate would result in a reduction in total research and development outlay of about $3.2 billion, or about 23 per cent. It appears, then, that on these assumptions the proportional drop in total research and development expenditure in the economy would be about half as great as the proportional cutback in military expenditure. . . .

COMPOSITION OF DEMAND

The preceding calculations did not take into account the significant differences in research and development for different industries of the civilian economy. Clearly, if civilian demand expands in such a way as to call forth a high level of output in the electrical equipment industry, for example, this would lead to a larger total national research and development effort than if civilian demand increased principally for, say, agricultural products. It therefore is useful to explore the effects of different compositions of increases in nonmilitary demand.

Leontief and Hoffenberg have estimated,* by input-output techniques, the increased sales levels of the various industries which would be induced by a $1 million increase in investment, consumption, military spending, and other final-demand categories. . . . My rough calculations indicate that $1 of consumption final demand generates 1.2 cents of research and development expenditure, a dollar of investment final demand about 4.5 cents of research and development spending, with the other Leontief-Hoffenberg nonmilitary . . . categories falling between these two . . . in their research and development impact. . . .

EMPLOYMENT VERSUS SPENDING

This estimate of the expenditure impact significantly overstates the impact of disarmament on employment of scientists and engineers. There are two reasons for this. First, expenditure on research and development covers a good deal more than the salaries of scientists and engineers. A good percentage (more than half) of the expense is for materials and equipment and the salaries of technical assistants and administrative people. In military research and development dollar hires only three quarters the number of re- ment which involves heavy materials outlay, the percentage of total research and development outlay attributable to salaries of scientists and engineers is significantly smaller than in nonmilitary research and development. It is estimated that the defense research and development dollar hires only three quarters the number of research and development scientists and engineers as the nondefense research and development dollar.

Second, . . . only about one third of our scientists and engineers are engaged in research and development (on a full-time equivalent basis). About two thirds of their time is spent on problems of production control and planning, administration, sales, and teach-

* W. Leontief and M. Hoffenberg, "The Economics of Disarmament," *Scientific American* (April 1961).

ing. In the defense industries, research and development scientists and engineers comprise a much larger share of the total number than in nondefense industries. It is estimated that approximately 50 per cent of the engineers and scientists in defense work are in research and development, while in nondefense work the figure is only 25 per cent.

Taking into account both [these factors,] . . . it can be calculated that the preceding calculations overstate . . . the impact of a compensated decline in defense spending on the employment of scientists and engineers. . . . [Although] a 50 per cent decline in defense spending would lead to a 23 per cent cutback in research and development spending, it would lead to only a 12 per cent cutback in employment of scientists and engineers.

SECTORAL IMPACT

The figures ground out by these [assumptions] . . . suggest, first, . . . a cutback in defense expenditure compensated by an increase in nondefense final demand will lead to a proportional reduction in research and development outlay somewhat less than half as great. Second, . . . a given proportional cutback in defense spending will result in a proportional cutback in employment of scientists and engineers about one quarter as great. It is worthwhile to look beneath the aggregative figures to try to get some feel for the organizations and industries which would be most affected.

In 1960, the . . . [DOD] financed about 75 per cent of the work done in government facilities, slightly more than 50 per cent of the work performed by industry, and about 25 per cent of the work performed by colleges and universities and other nonprofit institutions. If one half of the expenditure of the AEC is included, the figure for the universities and other nonprofits rises to about 35 per cent. Thus defense cutbacks would seem likely to fall with greatest proportional impact on government-owned facilities, with next greatest on industry, and least upon universities and other nonprofit centers.

Consideration of the type of work done for the DOD by these different sectors strengthens the conclusion that universities would not be hard-hit. It is likely that basic research projects financed by the DOD would not be cut back as much as research and development tied to weapons. . . . [Even if] defense spending for basic research is cut back, these projects would become prime candidates for nondefense support. . . . [Although] only about 3 per cent of DOD-supported work in industry is basic research, about 40 per cent of the work in colleges and universities financed by the DOD is. . . .* Thus, both because the DOD finances a relatively small share of research and development at the universities and because much of that work is basic research which is unlikely to be cut back drastically, the impact of disarmament on research and development at the universities should not be particularly great. . . .

A large proportion of DOD-financed work carried on by industry is closely tied to specific weapon systems, and thus is apt to be very sensitive to arms reduction. Somewhere around 85 per cent of it is development work. Moreover, the impact of disarmament on industry research and development is likely to be concentrated in a few industries. Of the DOD's industrial research and development spending, more than 50 per cent goes to the aircraft and parts industry and about 20 per cent to the electronics industry. Looked at in another way, the . . . [DOD] supports better than half of the research and development done in three industries—aircraft 85 per cent, electrical equipment about 60 per cent, and communications about 50 per cent—while in such industries as food, chemicals, petroleum, and primary metals, it provides less than 10 per cent of the funds.

The fact that military research and development has a different "mix" than nonmilitary research and development suggests that disarmament would affect the various scientific and technical professions very differently Unfortunately, the scientific and technical manpower data are much too aggregate to provide support for this conjecture.

The Workings of the Market

THE GENERAL FRAMEWORK

The previous analysis was based on given and assumed constant research and development-to-sales ratios. But before it is assumed

---

* It should be noted that the DOD supports a much smaller fraction of basic research than total research and development. Indeed, the DOD supports only about 15 per cent of the total basic research done in the United States. If AEC support is added, the figure comes to about 25 per cent. For this reason, as well as those stated above, the impact of disarmament is likely to be much less on basic research than on other kinds of research and development.

that the figures . . . provide a rough measure of the job for public policy, . . . we should examine how the market mechanism is likely to contribute to the solution. . . . In particular, how might research and development-to-sales ratios change in response to an excess supply of scientists and engineers [and a reduction in their salaries]?

The determinants of research and development spending have been under increasing study by economists. There is mounting evidence that, over the short run, the level of research and development spending can be reasonably well explained by . . . [assuming] firm managers act as if they have a target research and development-to-sales ratio, and that they try to reduce a discrepancy between this target . . . (or rule of thumb) and the actual . . . ratio. The widespread (but far from universal) existence of a "target" . . . ratio has been uncovered by NSF interviews. Norton Seeber has collected considerable evidence on this point and Edwin Mansfield has tested such a model statistically and found it quite reliable.*

But over relatively long periods of time, particularly when prices and technologies are changing, it seems likely that short-run rules of thumb also change. On the average, the rules of thumb . . . should change so as to move closer toward that which is optimal [in terms of profits]. . . .

. . . [Perhaps the orders of magnitude involved can be suggested by assuming that] a 1 per cent decline in research and development unit costs will lead to a 1 per cent increase in the quantity of resources applied to research and development.

. . . Earlier . . . it was suggested that a 50 per cent cutback in military expenditures would lead to approximately a 23 per cent cutback in research and development spending, holding research and development unit costs constant. The preceding analysis suggests that a 23 per cent reduction in research and development unit costs would enable the market itself to take up the slack. To restore research and development *employment* would require a cost reduction of less than 20 per cent.

* Seeber's work is as yet unpublished. Mansfield's results are published in *The Rate and Direction of Inventive Activity* (National Bureau of Economic Research, Princeton: Princeton University Press, 1962).

FACTOR SUBSTITUTION

The costs of research and development, however, include much more than the salaries of scientists and engineers. In fact, the salaries of scientists and engineers comprise only a little more than a quarter of total research and development costs in American industry. This makes it difficult to estimate the . . . [response] of research and development employment of scientists and engineers with respect to a cut in wage and salary levels. The crucial [question] . . . is . . . substitution between scientists and engineers and other research and development factors of production.

At one extreme, if research and development factor proportions are relatively fixed, in order to achieve an x per cent increase in employment of scientists and engineers the market will require a fall in the salaries of significantly more than x per cent, unless the costs of other research and development inputs fall also. However, if research and development factor proportions are relatively flexible, then the stickiness of other factor prices may actually help the employment situation for scientists and engineers. To gain an x per cent increase in employment will require a less than x per cent decline in salaries. Unfortunately, there exist almost no data from which either the . . . [possible] substitution or the likely market response of the cost of the other factors can be estimated.

THE DYNAMICS OF ADJUSTMENT

The dynamics of the adjustment mechanism, however, are likely to be relatively favorable. The target research and development-to-sales ratios are likely to be adjusted upward in response to a slack market for scientists and engineers. The recent work of Cyert and March* suggests that the decision rules established by a firm are likely to be relatively stable if they generate results which are satisfactory. However, if the results are less than satisfactory, the organization or individual tends to re-examine the decision rules and to search for improvement. . . .

* Richard M. Cyert and J. G. March, *A Behavioral Theory of the Firm* (Englewood Cliffs, N.J.: Prentice-Hall, Inc., 1963).

Let us assume that as other firms increase their research and development spending a firm which does not increase its own spending will experience a decline in market share. And the fall in market share is likely to, although it need not, be reflected in smaller profits. Then, if disarmament leads to an increase in the optimal research and development-sales-ratio, as soon as a few firms act to increase their spending, this will put pressure on other firms to reevaluate their own research and development decisions.

Firms under profit pressure may well be able to determine their appropriate research and development response by imitating the more successful firms; the firms which increased their research and development spending earlier. As Sidney Winter has pointed out in an unpublished paper, the economic system tends to enforce good decision rules not only by killing off inefficient firms but by providing models for them to imitate to become more efficient.** Norton Seeber and the . . . [NSF] have found considerable evidence that firms in an industry pay a considerable amount of attention to the research and development policies of the more successful firms.

Problems of Public Policy

EMPLOYMENT

Although scientists and engineers will probably be harder hit by arms reduction than any other occupational group (save military people), it is not likely that unemployment of scientists and engineers will be more than a very short-run problem. Research and development is one of the fastest-growing activities in our economy, despite some retardation in the last few years, and the employment of scientists and engineers is growing at a faster rate than employment of almost any other occupational group.

In the earlier analysis it was assumed that arms reduction would come suddenly and sharply, and the calculated cutbacks in spending and employment are, therefore, an upper bound. It can be shown that if the ratio of civilian research and development to civilian final demand does not decrease its rate of growth dramati-

** Winter's unpublished paper, "Economic Natural Selection and the Theory of the Firm," [also] points out some important ways in which "imitation" may mislead.

cally, then a phased disarmament program might not reduce total research and development spending at all but rather would (temporarily) retard its rate of growth.

If salaries are at all flexible, if the response of research and development employment to changes in salaries is reasonably great, and if scientists are reasonably mobile, this suggests that the impact of arms reduction on employment of scientists and engineers is likely to be more a temporary retardation of the rate of growth of salaries than significant unemployment.

However, in a situation where demand has shifted greatly, the federal government can play a very helpful role in oiling the adjustment mechanism. Programs might be developed to help scientists and engineers previously engaged in defense work to learn to tailor their training to the problems of civilian industry. Quite possibly something should be done to reduce the cost of moving, . . . [because] there is likely to be a significant shift in the geographical composition of demand. Making moving expenses fully tax deductible seems a reasonable step. Perhaps the government should go further and develop tax-credit schemes to facilitate mobility.

If more action is deemed necessary, then a step-up in the peacetime space program is ideally suited for the job. The industries involved, the locations, the skills are almost a perfect match for those which will be hit hardest by arms reduction. Whether an increase in the space program is justified on the basis of other criteria is another question.

WELFARE

As has been stated earlier, our concern about a cutback in research and development resulting from a reduction in defense spending transcends our concern with maintaining full employment. We tend to think (rightly) of research and development as an activity yielding a bountiful crop of external economies—as an activity to which the market will allocate too small a fraction of our resources in the absence of public action. If we take this point of view, our defense effort is yielding us a bonus by causing a larger research and development effort than we would have in the absence of our defense programs, and one of the real costs of arms reduction might be the shifting of resources away from research and development.

However, much of the discussion of the economic impact of our defense and space research and development efforts has tended to ignore the fact that the overwhelming percentage of defense research and development dollars is spent on work aimed at creating a specific new component or system for the military. Certainly this kind of research and development contributes far less to the advance of civilian technology than research and development concerned more directly with civilian problems.

The civilian economy obviously does gain some byproduct advantage from the research and development financed by defense agencies. But military research and development increasingly is exploring areas far away from those of clear relevance to the civilian economy. . . . [Although] it is difficult to measure the degree of civilian relevance, . . . clearly research on mildew-resistant fabrics for military use is much more likely to have immediate civilian application than research on nose cones. A very large percentage of the civilian applications of military research and development listed in the ORO study . . . [cited] earlier is of the "mildew-resistant cloth" type, and this type of research and development probably is a much smaller percentage of total military work today [than] before the Missile Age.

Indeed, the case can be made that in recent years the growth of military and space research and development has significantly retarded the growth of civilian research and development. Between 1954 and 1961, while the number of total scientists and engineers in research and development in industry grew at approximately a 10 per cent annual rate, the number financed by private industry out of their own funds and, presumably, involved principally on civilian programs grew at only one third that rate. There is considerable feeling among research and development directors that the growth of defense research and development, by bidding up salaries and by taking the cream of the new science and engineering graduates, has tended to reduce significantly the quantity and quality of research and development undertaken in civilian-created laboratories.

In any case, a significant increase in research and development resources could be used in the civilian sector, with large benefit to society. In many of the civilian industries, very little research and development is presently directed toward improving products and processes. . . . [Although] in the aircraft and parts industry and the communications and other electrical equipment industries (the industries accounting for more than 80 per cent of government research funds spent in industry) research and development spending exceeds 10 per cent of sales, for all other industries taken together the figure does not exceed 3 per cent. Increased research and development spending undoubtedly would yield high returns in many of these industries. The civilian economy would benefit especially from increased long-range research and experimentation with advanced technological possibilities of the sort that the research teams presently employed by defense industries have conducted so successfully. The freeing of these highly trained research resources for application to civilian technology would hold great promise for increasing the welfare of the American people.

In addition to the nonmilitary domestic use for research and development resources that would be freed by disarmament, these resources could be used to complement an expanded foreign aid program. Research and development might be focused on such problems as development of simple teaching machines and related communications equipment, techniques for overcoming aridity, efficient and low-cost transportation systems, cheap and reliable power sources, and other equipment and processes specially tailored to the resource and labor availabilities of the less-developed economies.

A disarmament program would provide an unmatched opportunity to review public policies toward nonmilitary research and development. For the first time in years we would be faced with a slack market for scientists and engineers. There are urgent needs for more research and development in areas where private incentives and financial capabilities are weak. Government support might be given to enlarged research programs in such fields as urban transportation and housing. Policies to encourage more basic research might be considered. The freeing of research and development resources could be one of the most important economic benefits of disarmament. Because the uses of the research and development resources which would be freed by disarmament are so important and so many, in this field, certainly, the economic benefits of disarmament would dwarf the problem.

HELPING COMMUNITIES ADJUST

Donald F. Bradford

Many cities and towns in the United States have already experienced the effects that would follow disarmament. They have suffered from cutbacks in particular defense programs or from closings of bases and installations, although the total defense budget was rising or stable. These areas are the victims of changing military technology or new efficiency measures. The Office of Economic Adjustment, in the U.S. Department of Defense, attempts to aid such communities make the transition to other kinds of activity. In this selection, the director of the Office of Economic Adjustment explains its work and the successes achieved. It was originally presented to the Subcommittee on Employment and Manpower of the Senate Committee on Labor and Public Welfare in November 1963. It is reprinted here in slightly abridged form. (Printed in Nation's Manpower Revolution, Part 7 [Washington, D.C.: USGPO, 1963], pp. 2483-88.) The title has been supplied by the editor.

. . . The origin [of the Office of Economic Adjustment] was Presidential concern over the effects of necessary defense actions. In his defense message of March 28, 1961, the President said:

I am well aware in many cases these actions will cause hardships to the communities and individuals involved. We cannot permit these actions to be deferred; but the government will make every practicable effort to alleviate these hardships, and I have directed the Secretary of Defense to take every possible step to ease the difficulties for those displaced.

Secretary McNamara, accordingly, established the OEA in May 1961. It is our task to mobilize the resources of the Department of

Defense [DOD] and with the help of other federal agencies, state and local governments, and community organizations, to assist communities and individuals to overcome the difficulties created by these changes. It is a small Office. Nevertheless it can bring many of the resources of the federal government to bear on a given problem. . . .

. . . The types of DOD action which cause impacts are: (1) base closures; (2) reorganizations of defense activities; and (3) changes in procurement programs. The impacted area varies from the isolated community to the metropolitan complex. The extent of the impact varies with such factors as the percent[age] of the total work force affected; the percent[age] of the manufacturing and/or federal work force affected; the size of the community; the population growth, the unemployment rate and the viability of the local economy. The types of alternatives that we can apply vary from personal consultation to the mobilization of applicable federal assistance.

Perhaps the best way to discuss these elements is to illustrate them by actual cases. Our best example of a successful recovery from a base closure is the story of Presque Isle, Maine. . . . Presque Isle Air Force Base was a Snark missile base. This weapon system became obsolete and as a result, deactivation of the base was announced on March 30, 1961, with a target date for closure on June 30, 1961. This was a severe blow to the city, located as it is in an isolated geographic region, and dependent upon a one-crop economy. Loss of the base meant loss of 1259 military and 268 civilian jobs, representing an annual payroll of $3.5 million. Local procurement amounted to $1.8 million annually, while city schools received $102,000 in federal impact funds. To a community of less than 13,000 people, the magnitude of the impact was obvious and, accordingly, we worked with the local leadership from the beginning.

The kinds of assistance applied by our Office in this situation were in accordance with our philosophy that each community is different, with its own strengths and weaknesses, its own hopes and aspirations. We do not believe in stereotype solutions. Rather, we seek to develop ideas and approaches tailored to the special needs and desires of each community, as evaluated by the community itself. Accordingly, our actions in Presque Isle included:

Appointment of a local DOD consultant;

Discussions at the state level in support of a vocational school and necessary funding;

Establishment of new procedures to prevent unnecessary dismantlement of facilities;

Air Force donation of $108,000 worth of machine tools and equipment for vocational training;

Assistance to the Air Force in solution of personnel and property problems;

Liaison with . . . federal agencies . . . in property-disposal matters;

Assistance in organization and conduct of the Aroostook County industrial seminar, including participation of a federal task force;

Serving as a Washington contact for the community on matters pertinent to the recovery program in relation to federal agency assistance.

In September 1963, [Assistant] Secretary Morris was . . . the principal speaker at Presque Isle's salute to new industry dinner, which climaxed a week of celebration, honoring the many new industries that had come to the city. This whole story is a thrilling account of the energies and talents of the people of Presque Isle to whom great credit is due for a remarkable job of recovery and growth.

Other communities with whom we have worked include Benicia, Calif[ornia]; Harlingen, Tex[as]; Greenville, S[outh] C[arolina]; Lake Charles, L[ouisiana]; Spokane, Wash[ington]; Tongue Point, Oreg[on]; Green Cove Springs, Fl[orida]; Decatur, Ill[inois]. We have also worked on problems associated with Camp Kilmer and Raritan Arsenal, N[ew] J[ersey]; and Rossford Arsenal, Ohio, to name only a few.

A second type of impact is that occasioned by reorganizations within the . . . [DOD]. As progress is made in improving the effectiveness and reducing the costs of defense programs, many employees are affected through realinements and consolidations. Our Office has worked closely with the personnel people to develop policies and techniques which go far to assuring opportunities for continuing employment in federal service and the location of job opportunities for those who wish to remain in the local area.

. . . [DOD] personnel officers are enthusiastic about the new policies issued July 24, 1963, in what is known as the "Department of Defense policy and program for stability of employment for career employees." Specific features of this program are:

Advance planning and notice to employees;

Payment of transportation and travel expenses for employees who must be relocated,

Priority referral and placement within the . . . [DOD] for employees being involuntarily separated,

Retraining of employees made surplus in their present positions. The success of any program is dependent upon its acceptance by those who must translate it into action. We are, therefore, especially pleased that our new personnel policies were developed in large part through the work, in actual impact situations, of both installations and headquarters personnel officers of the military services and the Defense Supply Agency.

The record indicates that these efforts have paid off. Placement figures for personnel at twenty-five . . . installations in this country affected by closure, reductions-in-force, and transfer of function to other locations, show that of a total of 13,769 people, only 2493 or 18 per cent were separated, and that 1750 or 70 per cent of these 2493 were first offered other employment; 8556 or 62 per cent were placed, mainly in federal jobs, and 2720 or 20 per cent elected to retire or found employment on their own. Stated another way, only 750 out of the 13,769 did not benefit directly from the personnel program. A 93-95 per cent assistance record is highly gratifying. The cooperation of the Civil Service Commission and other federal agencies has contributed to this record. Although we cannot count on continued results at this high rate, the results obtained justify confidence that the program is sound.

The third type of impact is that resulting from changes in procurement programs. Our experience in this area is limited compared to the other types of impacts, and our office has not worked directly with contractors. We have, however, worked with local leadership in Wichita and Long Island and the results have been good.

In 1961, after the decision not to extend the B-52 production program beyond the fall of 1962, the Office met with Wichita officials to discuss the situation. We found civic leaders confident that Wichita would absorb the impact and grow. We did join with them, however, in a comprehensive evaluation of Wichita's advantages and disadvantages, assisted by a representative of the [U.S.] Department of Commerce. The primary recommendation was to seek greater diversification of the economic base through strengthening the industrial development program and the graduate school program.

In addition, to acquaint Kansas businessmen with business opportunities in defense contracting and to enable them to explore firsthand the government's purchasing techniques and the requirements specified by government agencies for private contractors, . . . [the DOD] joined with the University of Wichita on July 8 and 9, 1963, in a procurement clinic in Wichita. The Army, Navy, Air Force, and Defense Supply Agency attended along with several civilian agencies of the government and provided individual counseling to Kansas businessmen on how to do business with the government. Several hundred businessmen attended the two-day conference and we understand that they found it to be a valuable experience.

The confidence of Wichita officials in the future of their city has been borne out by events. The unemployment rate has remained consistently below the U.S. average, peaking at 5.5 per cent in midwinter, and dropping to less than 4 per cent in the summer months of 1962 and 1963. The rate in September 1963 was 3.5 per cent, compared with the national average of 5.2 per cent. In Wichita, 3.5 per cent represents 4800 workers.

Meantime, during the past year, Wichita has witnessed the acquisition of new plants and expansion of existing industries. Other economic indicators are also up. For example:

Lear Jet, manufacturer of executive aircraft and electronics, starting from zero a year ago, now employs 400. The Coleman Co[mpany] has moved in a water-heater plant. There have been, altogether, twelve small industrial starts this year. Boeing is employing a sizable work force on B-52 modification and SATURN work. Cessna has added 120,000 square feet of floor space. Abbott Chemical Co[mpany] has made a capital expansion of $1.2 million. Retail sales are up 4 per cent this year. Bank clearings are up 6.9 per cent and postal receipts, 6.5 per cent. Building permits have been greater all year, both in number and value.

None of this is surprising in the light of Wichita's assets: a progressive civic leadership, an experienced and productive labor force, a high educational level, sound finances, excellent utilities, and a good educational system oriented to training displaced employees.

Wichita leaders believe the city has weathered a difficult readjustment and is on the upgrade but still has some distance to go before anyone can feel complacent. Wichita citizens are essentially do-it-yourselfers and are demonstrating that they can do.

The situation is different in large metropolitan complexes such as Long Island. The market conditions in the metropolis determine the pace of readjustment of any segment of the economy. Fortunately, Long Island is a growing and dynamic community, characterized by a diversified industrial labor market.

The downward trend in F-105 aircraft production at the Farmingdale, Long Island, plant of Republic Aviation . . . has already resulted in some curtailment of employment, which will become more serious . . . as production comes to an end. This, of course, will generate reemployment problems for many thousands of individual workers, but the plant is located in a large, rapidly growing area, which can be expected to provide many new job opportunities in the future. . . .

The Office of Economic Adjustment met with Nassau and Suffolk County civic leaders several times in the spring and summer of 1962, accompanied on certain occasions by representatives of other federal agencies, the Departments of Commerce and Labor, the Small Business Administration, and the Urban Renewal Administration, discussing the problems and pointing out available federal services.

As an outgrowth of these discussions a two-county advisory group was formed, "designed to coordinate efforts to sustain the strength and growth of the Long Island economy." Called the Nassau-Suffolk Economic Development Council, it includes as members senior officials of Long Island firms.

This organized, knowledgeable effort of local business interests is especially important in large metropolitan complexes. We in the . . . [DOD] know only one variable affecting the area—military work. In any large metropolitan economic system there are many other forces involved which affect the economic equilibrium. We ourselves do not have, and are not likely to have in the immediate future, the data needed to permit accurate forecasting of the consequences of changes in military contracting upon a sizable metro-

politan system. The larger the metropolis (or region), the greater
are the uncertainties in predicting systemwide effects stemming
from a single action. . . . [There are] related projects designed to
provide more precise data on the economic impact of current defense spending [and to] . . . use these data to attempt to project
the future impact of anticipated changes in defense procurement.

Recognizing the limited role that the Office of Economic Adjustment can play in these larger situations, and as an interim measure
pending the establishment of the more comprehensive program,
there are services that the Office of Economic Adjustment can
perform which will assist in easing short-term impacts from contract
changes in metropolises and regions. These will, at the same time
add to the store of knowledge necessary to the development of
more sophisticated systemwide programs. These are:

RECONNAISSANCE

We can identify some of the larger areas likely to be affected by
contract changes. This can trigger an on-site examination of available economic data, given the assistance of groups like the Nassau-
Suffolk Council. If impacts begin to be felt, the actual events can
then be monitored more intelligently, and effective remedies can be
recognized more readily. Good reconnaissance can lead to a sound
determination as to whether or not we should offer our services to
the community.

COORDINATION

In a large metropolis, one of the most important services that
we can perform is to help assemble local resources required to deal
with any major adjustment problem. The prestige of the . . . [DOD]
and other federal agencies is a powerful tool which we can employ
to bring together on the metropolitan level decisionmakers from all
sectors of the community.

EVALUATION

An essential part of any program is to learn from experience, and
feed back the experience into future programs.

. . . The following is a composite of what has been done in various situations.

The Office of Economic Adjustment has

Visited communities informally, conferring with local leaders, assessing the circumstances, and offering recommendations when feasible;

Assisted in the development of community plans with the help of community, state, and other federal representatives;

Organized federal task groups for formal visits to communities; dependent upon the community plan, representation by other federal agencies varies; . . .

Organized industrial seminars with the help of DOD Small Business specialists, the Small Business Administration, GSA [General Services Administration], the [U.S.] Departments of Commerce and Labor, and the community leadership;

Developed DOD policies, to facilitate transfer of DOD property in the community interest, placement, or retention of DOD employees;

Provided paid DOD resident consultant during the planning period, when desired by the community.

Other elements of the Office of the Secretary of Defense [OSD] have helped in many ways:

The . . . [DOD] joins the Small Business and other civilian agencies in conducting small business counseling conferences regularly throughout the United States. During the past year representatives of the military departments have participated in over 200 such local events generally sponsored by the chamber of commerce. These conferences are aimed at providing guidance to businessmen on how to do business with the federal government.

Defense specialists work with economic development commission personnel of the state to place defense contracts with competent firms in depressed areas. As you know, the Defense Appropriation Act prohibits the paying of any price differential to relieve economic dislocations; however, we do have a partial set-aside technique which enables firms in depressed areas to receive preferential consideration in obtaining the award of one half of the contract quantities by matching the lowest bid received on the unreserved portion of the contract which is advertised.

Manpower elements of OSD have revised personnel policies,

granted or arranged waivers, as necessary to reduce impacts upon DOD civilians.

Real estate and base utilization elements of OSD have provided early warning of projected changes in installation payrolls.

In addition, other OSD offices have provided comparable assistance to . . . [our] programs when problems, or requirements for data, fell in their areas of responsibility. . . .

An impacted community can

Organize itself, under local leadership, to meet the problem by working for early community acceptance of the DOD decision, and expedited development of a community recovery plan which will exploit the strengths and correct the deficiencies;

Obtain professional assistance from universities and comparable groups to analyze its potential for growth;

Establish necessary organizations to work for community improvements attractive to new businesses;

Publicize its resources and attractions;

Maintain a positive liaison with the Office of Economic Adjustment, . . . providing it with a running account of its ideas, problems, successes, failures, and needs; asking OEA immediately for assistance and information when problems are encountered which cause difficulty to the community.

I want to mention one very important result of inquiries . . . conducted by us in the communities. They stimulate a dialogue on a major issue. Our recent experience in Roswell, N[ew] M[exico], for example, was the result of concern that the community's economic base was overly dependent upon defense. Local leadership concluded that it was sound to seek diversification, even though the airbase located there is considered a hard core base for the foreseeable future. They asked themselves how long was the foreseeable future and concluded that five, even ten years was not too early to think about alternatives. This is a farsighted approach which other communities could do well to emulate.

It appears that such a dialogue is also worth consideration by certain metropolitan areas and regions. A possible subject might be: "What is an optimum industry mix, with particular reference to military intensity?" Obviously, there is no ready answer to this question. It would seem, therefore, that it deserves thoughtful examination.

In closing, I would like to return to Presque Isle. Secretary McNamara, in commenting on the effort there, has said:

What has happened at Presque Isle is important, in my judgment, for the nation at large. It demonstrates what a community can do to change a serious problem into an opportunity. It shows the potential of teamwork between local, state, and federal governments. It is confirmation of the adaptability and resiliency of our people and our economy.

PART IV

Changing Boundaries between Public
and Private

THE NEW PARTNERSHIP

J. Stephan Dupré and Sanford A. Lakoff

*The following is part of the concluding chapter, originally titled
"Policy and Politics," of the authors' book* Science and the Nation
*(Englewood Cliffs, N.J.: Prentice-Hall, Inc., 1962). In this excerpt,
they discuss one important development of the Cold War: the
changing roles of public and private institutions caused by government sponsorship of research and development in industry and the
university. An implication which might be drawn from the discussion is that the new partnership between public and private could
be extremely useful in easing the economic adjustments required by
disarmament. The book was written when both authors were members of the Department of Government, Harvard University; Professor Lakoff is still at Harvard, while Professor Dupré is now a
member of the Department of Political Economy, University of
Toronto.*

. . . C. P. Snow, in his typically provocative manner, has pro-
posed a distinction between the older Industrial Revolution and the
modern "scientific revolution." There are limitations to this charac-
terization, as there are to all attempts to classify and label segments
of history, but it is a useful one to bear in mind in reflecting upon
the American experience with science and technology in recent
decades.

This much is surely plain:

As the state of technology becomes more complex, economically advanced nations must spend a sizable part of their national income on behalf of immediate and long-range innovation. The result is that both security and welfare depend less upon sheer productive capacity and natural resources and more upon scientific research and development. Increasingly, science plays a crucial role in the economy, in military preparedness, and even in the quest for prestige that symbolizes the competition among the nations. In the United States, these new demands have led the government to expand its traditional concern for national development and welfare to include large-scale sponsorship of scientific research carried out by industry, the universities, and government agencies. In the process, government has naturally come to require the advice and judgment of scientists over a wide range of important policy questions. To this extent at least, America may be said to be experiencing the scientific revolution—as a continuation or concomitant of the Industrial Revolution.

However we designate these changes, we should not lose sight of them. In themselves and in the implications they bear for the direction of American government and politics, they are surely of serious historical significance. This is especially the case with respect to the two parallel lines of development that we have stressed in this study. As we have seen, government sponsorship of research has led to an unprecedented breach of the traditional wall between public and private institutions and to a similar breach of the line that is usually drawn between the policy-maker and the technical adviser. In the sponsorship of research, public and private institutions are linked in a partnership that seems to be permanent; in political decisions affecting science, technical advice and policy-making go hand in hand. These two developments lie at the heart of what may be called the American experience of the scientific revolution.

The traditional principles that are being altered by these developments are of course well-known, even to the point of considerable exaggeration. Politicians and publicists continue to exploit widespread fears either that government is crushing private initiative or that private interest dictates public policy. If there is any political cliché more popular than these it is the belief that in some dark way experts are "taking over" from both the government and private interests. The value of the experiences examined in this study lies not so much in the novelty of the problems they raise as in the opportunity they provide for a concrete and realistic examination of these issues so often obscured or colored by dogmatic interpretation. . . .

Surely it is striking that, both in the area of policy and in the area of politics, older, more dogmatic lines have been broken by new arrangements bringing greater cooperation without radical social reorganization. An inflexible boundary between public and private would have made impossible the revolution in government science. An unbending separation of technical and policy advice would have done incalculable harm to military planning. . . . If science and the nation have become interdependent but not indistinguishable it is because implicity and explicitly those who have shaped the relationship have recognized that cooperation is essential if free institutions and individual freedom are to continue to function successfully. They have therefore sought to answer a national need but at the same time to promote institutional pluralism and personal responsibility.

It would be folly, of course, to shut our eyes blindly to the difficulties and dangers of such readjustments simply because they strike a hopeful balance between traditional values and contemporary needs. In a partnership in which private and public ends coexist, or in which different public ends must compete, it is bound to be difficult to achieve universal satisfaction. If technical advisers become more authoritative than their knowledge warrants, or if only one set of advisers gains the confidence of the political leadership, the delicate balance can be rudely upset. . . .

PUBLIC AND PRIVATE: THE DIPLOMACY
OF PARTNERSHIP

. . . As a government spending program, science is now second only to military hardware procurement and Armed Forces personnel. It has become a fiscal giant that surpasses even agricultural price supports.

The bulk of federal science expenditure is being devoted to the support of military research and development performed by business firms. In the pursuit of national security through research and development, government and industry have developed a partnership without precedent. In a very real sense, this partnership has the net effect of making government more like business and business more like government.

Military research and development juxtaposes the traditional roles of government and industry. Through the cost-reimbursement contract, government assumes the classic business role of the entrepreneur, the financial risk-taker. On the other hand, private business, because of its research and managerial capacities, assumes a substantial role in shaping military and strategic policies. Moreover, . . . [because] government does not have the capacity to supervise closely every phase of weapons development, business acquires a joint administrative responsibility for the expenditure of public money. In subcontracting, this responsibility includes participation in such important public policies as fostering small business and giving aid to economically depressed areas. At several junctures, business assumes public functions, while government performs the task of innovator.

The altered roles of government and business are largely the result of technological requirements. The principles of the market economy that are embodied in fixed price contracting cannot be applied to the procurement of research. In research and development, uncertainty is so great and the financial stakes so high that business cannot afford the risks and government cannot supply all of the needed scientific and managerial skills.

When the automatic regulation of the open market can no longer be applied to government-business relations, the only remaining checks on abuse are administrative in nature. Administration is seldom easy and never automatic, but the development of its tools will determine the satisfactory operation of the partnership between government and business.

Although this partnership has been made to work with fair efficiency, possible abuses will remain a challenge to the administrative skills and the mutual goodwill of each of the partners. Neither side can afford to take undue advantage of the other. The government, through irrational and thoughtless budgetary cuts, can easily wreck carefully chosen industrial research teams. Excessive red tape and petty administrative annoyances can lengthen the time needed to bring projects to completion.

Because industry is not so closely subject to the public constituency as government, private abuses of public responsibility are always a great potential danger. Business firms are under constant temptation to pad the cost estimates on which their fees are based. They can use special knowledge acquired in publicly supported work to violate the canons of free competition. They can try to pressure the government into embarking on wasteful programs that will result only in public loss and private gain. In brief, the survival and the potential achievements of a government-business partnership depend on a delicate balance of trust and cooperation.

The challenge posed by this alliance between public and private institutions is no less in the relationship between government and universities than in that between government and business. Understandably, however, the terms of the government-university partnership are different. The function of the universities has always been to advance knowledge and educate men. As such, institutions of higher education have had as their goal not private gain but the advancement of learning. Until recently, they pursued their goal either as independent institutions or under the sponsorship of state governments.

Today, the relative independence of universities from the federal government has been rudely shattered. The government has embarked on a deliberate policy of heavy subsidy to university research, both in pure science and in applied fields related to defense and health. Contracts and grants by the thousands have invaded the campus. University administrators and scientists find themselves immersed in the legalistic world of "Circular A-21," matching grants, and secrecy regulations.

The government has decided that research is not the only public need to be fulfilled by universities; many more scientists and engineers must be educated to meet the requirements of a technologically advanced society. Accordingly, fellowships, loans, and facilities grants are beginning to have a profound effect on the teaching, as well as the research, side of the university equation. Furthermore, new programs of federal aid to primary and secondary schools will only have the net effect of increasing popular demand for university education. On all sides, universities now find themselves firmly constituted as important components of public policy.

The difficulties of a close partnership between government and universities are both numerous and dangerous. . . . [Although] universities are entirely preoccupied with education, the federal government pursues policies in many areas, of which education is but one. It is in the very nature of a university to be jealous of its independence and individuality. But . . . [because] the government must reconcile many different demands, some of which may often be in conflict with others, the delicacy of government-university relations is bound to be extreme. The principal danger is that the timeless values of higher education will be sacrificed for too immediate needs. Government can stifle intellectual inquiry through overly stringent administrative and security regulations. In legislating for spending programs without due regard to over-all educational needs, government can create financial problems that in the long run will seriously threaten university welfare.

On their side, universities run the risk of becoming passive and complacent. As important components of public policy, they now have a duty and a responsibility constantly to remind public officials of the special nature of higher education. In this they fail at their peril, for federal policies will not be tailored to truly educational needs unless universities act as vigilant partners.

The partnership of public and private, of government, business, and education, will not work to optimal capacity on its own. It can serve the nation with full efficiency only if each of the partners exercises the restraint, the diplomacy, and the cooperation that are the basis of sound alliances. In our examination of the workings of the partnership, we have occasionally noted where certain general improvements might be made. Are these improvements reasonably attainable? Only time will tell, but one condition stands out above all others. It is the very thread that links the partnership; namely, science itself.

Greater concern for the special nature of science can polish many of the rough edges of the public-private partnership. It can help free scientists of excessive red tape in their work. It can lead the government to formulate less arbitrary budgetary policies in military research and development. An effort to distinguish more carefully between research and production can reduce military lead times and stimulate greater competition among business firms.

In questions affecting universities, greater concern for science becomes greater concern for higher education. It can promote more basic research and more liberal administrative and financial policies. It underlines the necessity for comprehensive analysis of the total impact of manpower programs on educational institutions, on research and teaching.

It is only reasonable that science should hold the key to the success of a public-private partnership that has been created to satisfy technological needs. The partnership must survive if the nation is to achieve security and welfare, but it will remain a constant organizational challenge to responsible policy-makers.

PART V

The Dangers of Political Pressure

THE MILITARY-INDUSTRIAL COMPLEX

Dwight D. Eisenhower

This excerpt is the best-known part of President Eisenhower's last official address to the nation, delivered by television and radio on January 17, 1961. It warns of the possible dangers to liberty in the huge military-industrial complex which is made inevitable by the international situation. The excerpt is taken from the text of the speech as reprinted in The Department of State Bulletin *(Vol. 44, February 6, 1961, pp. 179-182). The title has been supplied by the editor.*

A vital element in keeping the peace is our military establishment. Our arms must be mighty, ready for instant action, so that no potential aggressor may be tempted to risk his own destruction.

Our military organization today bears little relation to that known by any of my predecessors in peacetime, or indeed by the fighting men of World War II or Korea.

Until the latest of our world conflicts, the United States had no armaments industry. American makers of plowshares could, with time and as required, make swords as well. But now we can no longer risk emergency improvisation of national defense; we have been compelled to create a permanent armaments industry of vast proportions. Added to this, 3.5 million men and women are directly engaged in the defense establishment. We annually spend on military security more than the net income of all United States corporations.

This conjunction of an immense military establishment and a large arms industry is new in the American experience. The total influence—economic, political, even spiritual—is felt in every city, every statehouse, every office of the federal government. We recognize the imperative need for this development. Yet we must not fail to comprehend its grave implications. Our toil, resources, and livelihood are all involved; so is the very structure of our society.

In the councils of government we must guard against the acquisition of unwarranted influence, whether sought or unsought, by the military-industrial complex. The potential for the disastrous rise of misplaced power exists and will persist.

We must never let the weight of this combination endanger our liberties or democratic processes. We should take nothing for granted. Only an alert and knowledgeable citizenry can compel the proper meshing of the huge industrial and military machinery of defense with our peaceful methods and goals so that security and liberty may prosper together.

Akin to and largely responsible for the sweeping changes in our industrial-military posture has been the technological revolution during recent decades. In this revolution, research has become central; it also becomes more formalized, complex, and costly. A steadily increasing share is conducted for, by, or at the direction of the federal government.

Today the solitary inventor, tinkering in his shop, has been overshadowed by task forces of scientists in laboratories and testing fields. In the same fashion, the free university—historically the fountainhead of free ideas and scientific discovery—has experienced a revolution in the conduct of research. Partly because of the huge costs involved, a government contract becomes virtually a substitute for intellectual curiosity. For every old blackboard there are now hundreds of new electronic computers.

The prospect of domination of the nation's scholars by federal employment, project allocations, and the power of money is ever-present and is gravely to be regarded.

Yet, in holding scientific research and discovery in respect, as we should, we must also be alert to the equal and opposite danger that public policy could itself become the captive of a scientific-technological elite.

It is the task of statesmanship to mold, to balance, and to integrate these and other forces, new and old, within the principles of our democratic system—ever-aiming toward the supreme goals of our free society.

PLANNING FOR PROSPERITY

Norman Cousins

*In this essay the author takes the view that the shutdown of ob-
solete military installations should be hailed for the opportunities
it presents, rather than being lamented and opposed by political
lobbying. Norman Cousins is the editor of* Saturday Review, *and
this article appeared as an editorial in the December 5, 1964 (Vol.
47, p. 32), issue of the magazine, just after the U.S. Department of
Defense announced that a number of military bases and installations would be closed. Copyright © 1964, by Saturday Review, Inc.,
and reprinted by its permission.*

The owner of a small delicatessen in Brooklyn, New York, received prominent newspaper attention last week when he told his
Congressman and the press of the severe hardships that would be
imposed as a result of the government's decision to shut down the
Brooklyn Navy Yard. His cry of pain was only one of many thousands throughout the country in response to the order suspending
operations at obsolete or marginal military installations. Meanwhile, Congressmen and other officials of the affected areas registered their protests with the [U.S.] Department of Defense. It
might be noted in passing that in the recent election campaign
many Senators and Representatives sought to make political capital
out of their ability to obtain, save, or prolong defense spending in
their areas. Even Senators who have a reputation for opposing large
military budgets have made strenuous efforts, often successfully, to
retain or restore defense plants in their states.

The plight of the Brooklyn delicatessen owner, and others like
him, was real enough. But that is beside the point. The point is
that the most powerful lobby in American history is now at work

in behalf of what is in many respects a multibillion-dollar boon-doggle. It makes little difference if a defense plant is manufacturing equipment for which there is no longer practical use, or if the march of military technology has outmoded particular weapons and their integral parts. All that matters, apparently, is that arms spending means jobs or improved business.

After the First World War, writers like Philip Noel-Baker and Frank C. Hanighen* attracted widespread attention and provoked popular indignation with their contention that the war was brought on, at least in part, because of private concerns that lobbied for and profiteered in arms. The principal lobby today behind the arms race comes not just from the military or from manufacturers but from everyday people, labor unions, small shopowners, and congressional and local officials who are supremely vulnerable to economic and political pressure.

It is important to identify this lobby not just for historical purposes but as a matter of accurate contemporary labeling. No local storm is as great as the one that is stirred up by a report that defense spending in that area is about to be reduced. And those who recognize a specific danger in the mounting arms race will be misdirecting their energies if they address themselves solely to the military establishment. Indeed, for efficiency purposes alone, the military would like to discontinue many outmoded and cumbersome installations but are virtually forced to keep them going because of congressional pressure.

We are not arguing here that the hardships imposed by military shutdowns are not real. The laborer or the shopkeeper whose income is cut off cannot be expected to exult or do a victory dance, whatever the nature of his work. It is natural to expect that a man who has been wedded to a job for twenty years will fight to keep that job. But at least let us correctly identify this situation, if only to be in a better position to address ourselves to the human side of the problem.

Over the past twenty years, the occupants of the White House, whether Democratic or Republican, have frequently spoken of the opportunity offered by a cutback in military expenditures. For

* Philip Noel-Baker, M.P., *The Private Manufacture of Armaments*, Oxford University Press, 1937); H. C. Engelbrecht and F. C. Hanighen, *Merchants of Death*, Dodd, Mead, 1934).

example, it would be pointed out that the cost of a single bomber, if saved, could build a school or a hospital or a community center or so many miles of new road. Also, experts like Seymour Melman of Columbia University have demonstrated how armament plants can be converted into essential nonmilitary production. And public officials like Senator George McGovern of South Dakota have developed detailed plans for reconversion.

The time has come to put these reconversion plans into operation. We assume that the concept of peacetime equivalents was seriously advanced; very well, let it now be applied. When factory orders are discontinued or sharply reduced, new products can be adopted, in line with the detailed recommendations advanced by reconversion task forces. When the government decides to shut down a military installation, let it also make available the resultant savings for new prospects in the area affected.

It may be argued that the government lacks authority for applying economic equivalents—despite all the oratory about the need to apply military savings for peacetime purposes. True enough. But this would seem to make it imperative that proper authority be provided. We should suppose that many of the Senators and Congressmen who are doing their utmost to protect their areas against economic dislocation would recognize the need for legislation to empower the government to undertake reconversion or assist communities in such useful projects as will sustain and possibly even expand the area economy.

What we are trying to suggest is that a situation the nation has been hoping for these past two decades may be eventuating sooner than most people think. Increasingly, the nation may be in a position to take energies and resources now going into armaments and put them into the making of a better America. Instead of lamenting the shutdowns, we ought to be hailing them—both for the improved peace prospects they symbolize and for the economic opportunities they offer. In any case, we ought to be able to find something better to do with empty hands than to turn them to the manufacture of mass murder weapons

SUGGESTED READINGS

Benoit, Emile. "The Propensity to Reduce the National Debt out of Defense Savings," *American Economic Review*, LI, 2 (May 1961), 455–59.

Benoit, Emile, and Kenneth Boulding (eds.). *Disarmament and the Economy* (New York: Harper & Row, Publishers, 1963).

Bolton, Roger E. *Defense Purchases and Regional Growth* (Washington, D.C.: The Brookings Institution, forthcoming).

Fulton, Joseph F. "Employment Impact of Changing Defense Programs," *Monthly Labor Review*, LXXXVII, 5 (May 1964), 508-17.

Gilpatric, Roswell. "Our Defense Needs: The Long View," *Foreign Affairs*, XLII, 3 (April 1964), 366-78.

Henkin, Louis (ed.). *Arms Control: Issues for the Public*, American Assembly (Englewood Cliffs, N.J.: Prentice-Hall Inc., Spectrum Book S-AA-4, 1961).

Hitch, Charles, and Roland McKean. *The Economics of Defense in the Nuclear Age* (Cambridge, Mass.: Harvard University Press, 1961).

Isard, Walter, and James Ganschow. *Awards of Prime Military Contracts by County, State and Metropolitan Area of the United States, Fiscal Year 1960* (Philadelphia: Regional Science Research Institute, n.d.).

Lebergott, Stanley (ed.). *Men Without Work: The Economics of Unemployment* (Englewood Cliffs, N.J.: Prentice-Hall Inc., Spectrum Book S-105, 1964).

Leontief, Wassily W., and Marvin Hoffenberg. "The Economic Effects of Disarmament," *Scientific American*, CCIV, 4 (April 1961), 47-55.

Melman, Seymour (ed.). *Disarmament: Its Politics and Economics* (Boston: The American Academy of Arts and Sciences, 1962).

Salant, Walter, *et al. The United States Balance of Payments in 1968*, Chapter VII (Washington, D.C.: The Brookings Institution, 1963).

Schelling, Thomas C., and Morton Halperin. *Strategy and Arms Control* (New York: Twentieth Century Fund, 1961).

Steiner, George A. *National Defense and Southern California, 1961-1970*
(Los Angeles: Committee for Economic Development Southern California Associates, 1961).

U.S. Arms Control and Disarmament Agency. *Blueprint for the Peace
Race* (Washington, D.C.: USGPO, 1962).

————. *Economic Impacts of Disarmament* (Washington, D.C.:
USGPO, 1962).

————. *The Economic and Social Consequences of Disarmament* (Washington, D.C.: USGPO, 1964).

U.S. Congress, Joint Economic Committee. *Background Material on
Economic Aspects of Military Procurement and Supply: 1964,* Joint
Committee Print (Washington, D.C.: USGPO, 1964).

————. *Impact of Military and Related Civilian Supply and Service Activities on the Economy,* Hearings (Washington, D.C.: USGPO,
1964).

————. Senate Committee on Labor and Public Welfare. *Convertibility
of Space and Defense Resources to Civilian Needs: A Search for
New Employment Potentials, Selected Readings in Employment and
Manpower,* Vol. II, Committee Print (Washington, D.C.: USGPO,
1964).

————. *Nation's Manpower Revolution,* Hearings, Parts 7-9 (Washington, D.C.: USGPO, 1964).

U.S. Department of Defense. *The Changing Patterns of Defense Procurement* (Washington, D.C.: Office of the Secretary of Defense, 1962).

————. *Five-Year Trends in Defense Procurement: Fiscal Year 1958–
Fiscal Year 1962* (Washington, D.C.: Office of the Secretary of Defense, 1963).

The American Assembly Series

Classics in History Series